To "mom" —
love,
Ken

SO MANY HOTELS, SO LITTLE TIME

BY KENNETH VINCENT

Strategic Book Group

Strategic Book Group
P.O. Box 333
Durham CT 06422
www.StrategicBookClub.com

ISBN 978-1-61204-250-3

Introduction

Join me in a reminiscent romp through the forty-six years of my hotel management career that spanned from 1954 to 2000. I will take you on a journey through a world of funny, scary, and bizarre events, which will even plunge you into the seedy underworld. I show what it takes behind the scenes to provide you with a clean, safe, and comfortable place to rest your head, and to provide you with sustenance.

While I struggle to make our hotel profitable, you will join me as I dine with royalty and presidents. You will share my experience as I meet with prostitutes, and deal with snakes and pigs. It is all a part of the life of a hotel manager.

"Life is a Cabaret, old chum, come to the Cabaret." – *Cabaret,* 1972.

DEDICATION

I dedicate this book to my family members who endured the adventure, and to the thousands of employees and peers who worked with me over the years. A very special thanks to my wife, Christina, who without her help and encouragement this would never have gone to print.

Ken Vincent

About the Author

Mr. Vincent worked his way through high school and college, beginning as a bellboy.

He graduated from Oklahoma State University with a BS in hotel and restaurant management. He took summer courses at Cornell University and taught extension courses for the American Hotel/Motel Association, offered through Michigan State University.

During his career, he managed over one hundred hotels, formed eight companies, and owned two hotels. He has also conducted seminars about hotel management, investing, and motivation.

Mr. Vincent is also a published poet and he has written articles about hotel management contracts.

TABLE OF CONTENTS

CHAPTER I

WHY ME, LORD?

He stood before the pearly gates,
His face was scarred and old.
He stood before the pearly gates,
For admission to the fold.

"What have you done," St. Peter said,
"To gain admission here?"
"I've been a hotel man, Sir
For many and many a year."

St. Peter turned and rang the bell,
The gates swung open wide.
"Come in and choose your harp, my friend,
You've had your share of Hell!"

What caused me to write that? I hope that as you read the following pages, you will come to understand. Life managing a hotel can be, and often is, Hell.

But it will define you, and many of your opinions and theories, or it will break you.

Most everyone who has stayed at a hotel or resort has envied the manager, even if he or she is never seen, and they usually are not. (It is unfortunate that most guests get no exposure to any management personnel in a hotel higher than a desk clerk, a hostess in the dining room or perhaps a section housekeeper.) What is not to envy? Here a man or woman has a cushy job sitting in an air-conditioned office, with a restaurant, a fully stocked bar, a swimming pool, and a staff of people to respond to his every beck and call. Some of the luckier managers even have a beach, golf course, or tennis court in their little sphere of Heaven. Maybe all the above, with an exercise room tossed into the bargain.

I heard the following one day while inspecting my little piece of Heaven.

"I could do this," a guest said to his wife as he slathered on some more suntan lotion by the pool.

"Do what?" she asked.

"Manage a hotel like this."

"What do you know about running a hotel?" was her immediate response.

"How hard can it be? You hire a bookkeeper, a cook, a housekeeper, a maintenance man, and let them hire a few people to help them. Then you order lunch in your office, maybe with a glass of wine, and play a computer game."

"Well, I think there must be more to it than that," she said as she took a sip of her rum punch.

Having managed well over one hundred hotels, I can tell you with some considerable conviction that there is more to it than that.

This book will not teach you how to manage a hotel. It will not teach you much of anything, except that managing a hotel is not the cushy job that it appears to be. Perhaps it will teach you some things you didn't know about hotels, or even better yet, it may entertain you. It is really the saga of one man's forty-six year trek through the Hell, and Heaven, commonly called the hotel industry.

A note here about your personal beliefs may be in order. If you have religious, moral, or ethical issues with drinking, smoking, sex, drugs, murder, or other crimes, you may want to avoid a career in hotel management. It is very awkward to entertain the mayor over dinner, and order a ginger ale for yourself when he orders a scotch and water. Of course, if lying doesn't bother you, then you can always make up an excuse such as, "I can't mix alcohol with my medication."

Managing a hotel is fun. It is challenging. It is sometimes scary. It is hard work with long hours. It is demanding of one's emotions. It is frustrating. It is rewarding. It is exciting. It is also Hell.

After I graduated from a major university with a degree in hotel and restaurant management, I got a job as a management trainee with a major chain of hotels. I quickly learned that I didn't know squat about managing a hotel. I also learned that what they had taught me in hotel school was largely worthless in the real world. In my forty six-year career, no one ever asked me about the chemical formula for what happens to an egg yolk when you boil the egg. (This is not to say that a person should not go to college.) So, just what does the guest by the pool need to know? Well, for starters, he will need to know something about the following:

- Sales, advertising, public relations, and marketing
- Food purchasing, preparation, and service
- Butchering and cuts of meat and meat quality
- How vegetables, fruits, and meats are graded
- Bar pricing, purchasing, and drink preparation
- Wines
- Security of building, guests, and personnel
- How many ways there are to steal from a hotel and about the types of people that do it

- Accounting
- Financial analysis
- Maintenance of building, grounds, amenities, and a lot of diverse equipment
- Front desk operation and room price management
- Computers and phone systems
- Interior design and decorating
- Building plans and blue prints
- Housekeeping, laundry, and cleaning supplies and chemicals
- Hotel laws and liquor laws in your city and state
- OSHA rules
- Employment laws
- Real estate and employment taxes
- Inventory control
- Unions and union organizing
- Writing and pricing menus
- Contract negotiations and legalities
- Construction and renovation
- Insurance:
  property
  employee health
  workman's comp
  liability
  auto
- Handling guest problems and complaints
- Cost control of labor, food, beverage, utilities, etc.
- Catering
- People and what makes them tick
- CPR can be helpful too, as is public speaking.

You see, the problem is that you are not running a business. You are running several diverse businesses mostly housed in a single building. (I say mostly, but we had one hotel where we delivered lunches to offices via bicycle.) These businesses include short-term housing rental, housekeeping services, wedding planning, convention planning, á la carte restaurant operations, catering, banquet planning, bar operations, etc. Any one of these businesses can be a carrier in itself.

While I don't mean the above to be a complete list of what you need to know, it does show that managing a hotel is not just a matter of lounging around the pool and two martini lunches. There will be more about many of the above subjects later.

By way of example of what can interrupt your "two martini lunch by the pool," I will cite the following events.

It was a screaming hot August afternoon. The temperature had been over 100 degrees since 10 a.m. At about 4 pm, I received a call from a businessman in an office in the building across the alley from my hotel. He said, "I hate to bother you with this, but I think I can see two shoes sticking out of a vent on the roof over your coffee shop."

I went to the roof to find two feet sticking out of the vent and a smell that brought me to my knees. I called the fire rescue squad and the police. After cutting a section of the roof away, the rescue team extracted a man's very bloated body. He had apparently been a guest and had taken a header out of the sixteenth floor window, wedging himself head first into the exhaust duct. Yes, suicides are common in hotels, usually by jumping or by gunshot.

In this same hotel, the desk clerk called me in the middle of the night to inform me that the coffee shop kitchen was on fire. I asked him if he had notified the assistant manager and the fire department. He informed me that he had called both. (Both the assistant manager and I lived in the hotel.) I grabbed some clothing and went to the scene to meet the fire department coming in the front door. After the crises had passed, I realized that I had not seen my assistant manager. I went to his suite to find that he was still in bed. I fired him. Like in the old sailing ships, a fire is the most feared of disasters in a hotel.

On another occasion, I learned that a guest elevator was stuck between the fourth and fifth floors with three people in it. I went to the fifth floor, opened the elevator door with an emergency key, and got on top of the elevator. By opening the ceiling hatch, I could help the people out of the car and into the hall. As the last trembling person reached the safety of the fifth floor hall, the elevator brakes gave way and the car dropped four floors with me riding on the top. After this event, I could have used a couple of martinis, stirred not shaken, I felt shaken enough for both the martinis and myself.

While these types of events are not daily occurrences, they are more frequent than two martini lunches and sipping rum punch by the pool.

I have stated that I got a hotel and restaurant management degree, but that is not how or when I got into the hotel business. Perhaps a bit more about my background will help in understanding the theories to come in later chapters.

I actually got into the hotel business at age fourteen as a bellboy. In three months, I was promoted to bell captain, and I got my first taste of supervising employees. In my teen years, I gained experience working on the front desk, doing the night audit, working in accounting, and a smattering of experience in housekeeping and maintenance. By my junior year in high school, I was working sixty hours per week and in love with the hotel business.

During my time as a bell captain, I began to learn about people. I learned, among other things, that people love their names. It is something that is just their's. I learned that if I called a guest by name my tips doubled or tripled. By my senior year in high school, I was making more money than anyone else in the hotel, except the General Manager, even though my pay rate was only twelve cents per hour.

I spent three years attending the local state teachers college, getting my basics out of the way in preparation for transferring to a university where I could get a hotel degree. One of the courses that I needed to take at the teachers college was a basic food preparation class. (The food prep courses that I would have to take later were in a sequence, and this course would save me a full semester later.) The home economics department at the college offered the class, and it was a popular elective for girls. I was the first male ever to enroll in the class. The first day of class, the teacher said that all the students must wear a white dress and a hair net. Oh, great! I had a little trouble seeing myself sashaying across campus in a white dress and hair net. Of course, the girls in the class all looked at me and snickered, not very discreetly I might add. After class, I approached the teacher about this issue. She agreed that I could wear white pants, a white shirt, and a white paper hat. Whew! I might add that probably the only reason I passed the class was that I was the only student that would empty the mousetrap.

In the university, to earn a hotel degree I took classes in:

I Accounting
I Blue print reading
I Architecture
I Interior design and decorating
I Table settings
I Catering
I Butchering beef, swine, sheep, ducks, fish and chickens
I Grading of meat, fruit and vegetables
I Chemistry
I Building maintenance
I Menu planning
I Sanitation
I Personnel management

▌ Legal issues
▌ Contract organization and negotiations
▌ Food preparation

After college, I held numerous management positions in several cities. I eventually started a hotel management company as a subsidiary of a parent company, and later took the management company private. More on all this later. However, I should note here for those who are interested in a career of hotel management, you will need to be willing to move a lot. Not doing so because of ties to family or community will stifle the career. I moved twenty-three times in my career. At one point, my mother counseled me to stop moving so much. People would think I had a drinking problem and couldn't hold a job. If you are not willing to move, then consider managing a clothing store, a hardware store, or becoming a lawyer.

Whatever you do, do it because you love it. I can think of nothing more tragic that having to go to work every day to a job you hate and dread.

With this as a basic understanding, we will move along to more about hotels.

CHAPTER II

WHAT IS A HOTEL?

A hotel is a hotel is a hotel. Right? Wrong.

There are several types of hotels, each having a unique position in the market place and each having problems that are common to that type of hotel. Of course, each individual property has its own set of opportunities and problems that are not common to others of that class. The guest by the pool will need to know this if he is in fact serious about managing a hotel.

At the risk of over generalizing, we can categorize hotels as Bed and Breakfast (B&B), Motels, Hotels, and Resorts. We will ignore such variations as residential hotels, seasonal properties, etc.

A B&B is small. Generally, they are converted large old houses located in rural areas, in small towns, or at the outskirts of medium-sized cities. However, we actually managed one that was a converted cotton warehouse and one that had been a small dorm of a college. Usually they have three to ten rooms and often some of the rooms share a bath down the hall. They offer a breakfast as part of the room rate. There is no other food service in the facility, but many of them do offer a happy hour, or an honor bar. These facilities offer a most pleasant stay, with the host or hostess giving personal attention to the guest, and creating a lasting pleasant memory. Or else, they are the stay from Hell. Choose wisely, hopefully with the recommendation from someone who has stayed there. My wife and I have stayed at both groups.

These facilities are typically owner operated, but may have absentee ownership. Many of the people I have known in the hotel industry (and not a few who are not in the industry) dream of owning and operating their own B&B. May God help me if I ever have such a dream (nightmare). No other type of hostelry is as completely demanding. You-hopefully a couple-have to do everything. You might have a maid, who may or may not show for work, and a breakfast cook, who may or may not show for work. Of course, you have to pick up the slack if one or both do not show for work, or if someone comes to work after a few drinks. You must also do all the buying and receiving of food, liquor, cleaning supplies, paper goods, room supplies, replacement linens, etc. You must also be available to take reservations at all hours of the day and night, check guests in and out, do the bookkeeping, and the maintenance of the building, its grounds, and equipment. Worked into these duties you must also play host/ hostess to your houseguests, for that is what they are. You need to be available and visible. You need to see to their every need and comfort, give directions and suggestions about local events, restaurants, and places to visit. By treating your guests as personal houseguests, they can even suck you into their personal issues. I know of one case where the managing couple had to break up a fight between a husband and wife at 3 a.m. and then spent the rest of the night counseling them. The owner/manager of a B&B is on deck fourteen-plus hours a day, seven days per week.

We spent a week at one B&B in New Orleans where the cook came to our room to get my wife out of the shower when he learned that she had opted to skip breakfast. He took that as a personal insult.

Motels are typically highway locations meant to serve the traveler who is passing through an area. At least that was the original intent. As I recall, the first chain of motels was Quality Courts, which eventually became Quality Inns and is now Choice Hotels. As President Eisenhower developed the interstate system in the 1950s, highway travel became very popular for families on vacation, businessmen, etc. (there were few traveling business-women in those days). Holiday Inns was born. A rash of other brand names quickly followed these motels, and in a few years, there was a motel at half of the interstate exits in the country. Motels in their original concept were pretty much "plain Jane" operations. They offered clean and convenient rooms. However, as competition increased and guest demands became more evident, motels became subject to what I call "creeping amen-ities." What is a creeping amenity? (It is not mice, bed bugs, or cockroaches.)

Say, for example, that you have a basic motel at exit 10. I build a newer one at exit 12. I begin to get some of your business. You put in a pool to get your business back. I put in a pool and cover it for year-round use. You put a coffee pot in each room. I put a coffee pot in each room and offer a free continental breakfast. You put in a larger bar of soap. I match that and add shampoo and cream rinse, etc. It is understood that these creeping ameni-ties also ratchet up room rates.

Now, the designation between motels and hotels has become very blurred. Many, if not most, motels now offer a fairly full range of services, including a pool, exercise room, breakfast of some sort, one or more meeting rooms, computer connections in every room, free local phone calls, and often more. The brand name does not even give you a clue. Many of the original "motel chains" now have full-service hotels of several hundred rooms each under their brand. We managed two full-service Holiday Inns of 450 rooms each. Plus, traditional "hotel chains" like

Sheraton and Hilton are now in the motel business. To further blur the classic definitions, most major brands now have "all suite properties." The one thing that I would still use to classify a facility as a motel is a highway or interstate location. They have a very high rate of one-night stays as people pass through the area.

Hotels have historically been downtown locations, largely serving meetings, conventions, and business travelers. They have been full service facilities, often with multiple restaurants, bars, an exhibit center, various sized meeting rooms, and huge ballrooms. I once managed a hotel that had 750 rooms, a larger exhibit hall than the city convention center, a ballroom that could seat 3,000, three restaurants, and three bars. Two of these facilities offered live entertainment. That was not the largest hotel at the time, by far. A hotel, because of the mix of clientele, has its own unique set of problems. You will learn more about this along the way.

As an historical footnote, many early hotels were built, owned, and operated by the railroads in the time that rail travel became the rage. During the railroad era, the Harvey Girls concept was born out of necessity. Many of the more remote depots not only had no hotel, they had no restaurant either. When the train stopped so the steam engine could refill the boiler with water and take on coal or wood for fuel, the passengers wanted to stretch their legs and get something to eat. The Harvey Girls were a small army of women, all dressed in starched black and white uniforms, and well trained. They provided good food, and fast efficient food service at these stops, either in the railroad's hotel or in a wing of the depot. Fred Harvey hired professional chefs to offer such items as beef Stroganoff and chicken Vesuvius. These entrees could be expected in Chicago or New York City in the 1880s, but they were a rare treat in stops such as Ash Fork, Arizona, and Trinidad, Colorado. I believe the last two railroad hotels have now changed hands. Perhaps two of the more famous were the Roosevelt Hotel (1750 rooms) in New York City, and the Greenbrier in West Virginia. eventually, the Pullman dining cars replaced the need for the Harvey Girl stations

My first job as a bellboy was in a ninety-room former railroad hotel, though by then, the Santa Fe Line no longer owned it.

Resorts are, largely, full-service hotels with more recreational facilities and are not usually located in the center of a city. They may offer one or more beaches, pools, golf courses, and tennis courts. They may include a marina, and an exercise room, sometimes with personal trainers, and a spa. We even managed one with an FAA-licensed airport and another with a casino. Both resulted in a significant learning curve for management. If that were not enough to separate them from hotels as a group, the clientele would. Resorts are destination hostelries where people go to vacation, albeit sometimes as a part of a group or convention. An interesting variation in recent years is the all-inclusive resort. That means the guest pays one price for a given period and has free access to not just a room, but all food, bar beverages, and recreational facilities. Most of these are in off shore locations. Another variation is "clothing optional" beach or pool. As you can imagine, those add another whole dimension to the hotel manager's problems.

We managed one resort that had a topless pool outside the wing of meeting rooms. I quickly learned that to keep the staff focused on the meeting, and not on the pool scenery, I had to keep the drapes closed. We also had a tough time keeping our graphic artist focused on the needs of a photo shoot for a brochure, instead of the girls at the pool. He went through five times more film than was needed for the brochure pictures.

But, that is enough about your basic education regarding hostelries. Let us say for example, that your rich daddy is tired of being a landowner and wants to build a motel for you to manage. Where do you build it?

Well, let me tell you where not to build it. Don't build it across the interstate from three others. The theory behind building one next to the competition is that if there are three of them, there must be a lot of business in that location. However, it is very likely that one, if not all three, of the properties are in serious trouble and your fourth one will not fare any better.

Don't build it in a cornfield. Yes, I actually had a man who proposed to build a 200-room motel in the middle of what had been his cornfield. His theory was that since it was on a rise in the field it had great visibility from the interstate. (It didn't seem to matter to him that the nearest exit was three miles away via a dirt road.) He also argued that there was plenty of land for a pool and parking. His crowning theory was that he had traveled a lot with his kids as they grew up and so he didn't see why they couldn't manage it. As tactfully as possible, I told him that he was confusing his ass with an elephant and that he should stick to growing corn. He built it anyway, and had his three kids managing it. When it didn't work, he decided that it was just too small, so he added another 100-room wing and some meeting rooms. I think the highest occupancy he ever achieved in a given month was 11% and that was when he had his family reunion there. When the bank foreclosed on his mortgage, they called me to manage it. I declined.

Why did the bank finance it in the first place has to be a question that comes to mind. Well, there are accounting firms that will do a feasibility study to see if a location is desirable and will support a facility. Since the proposed owner is paying for the feasibility study, the firm is likely to say good things about the plan. (Why haven't banks figured this out yet?) Such a report was the basis of financing the project, not to mention the fact that the man had run a lot of money through the bank over the years. If your daddy gets a feasibility study from one of those firms, go to the nearest fireplace and use it as tender to start a fire. I have never seen a feasibility study that was worth the paper it was written on.

I looked at another motel that was doing poorly, but it was built at an interstate exit in what should have been a great location. The problem was there was no entrance ramp back onto the interstate at this interchange. Talk about no repeat business.

I also studied a 300-room motel that was running at ninety percent occupancy, but losing large amounts of money. When I dug into their finances, I discovered that the owner didn't count 200 of the 300 rooms in his motel as available. He was actually running only at thirty percent occupancy.

You can't judge a book by its cover is truism. I went to meet a developer in North Carolina once. He had plans to build a 400-room city hotel. When I got off the plane, he collected me and we got into a ten-year-old Ford pickup with a missing fender. He took me to his office, a cement-block building with two rooms and metal furniture. I was now convinced that this was going to be a wasted day and airline ticket. On the way back to the airport, he drove me through a very large housing development. He had sold 300 lots, built the houses, and carried the mortgages on all of them. Then he showed me his two fifteen-story office buildings and his Learjet. As he dropped me off at the Delta counter, he said, "By the way, I never take on debt, so my hotel has to be an all cash development." However, the hotel never got built due to some developing health problems of the developer. I did learn though that things are not always as they appear.

So with that behind us, let us look at who owns hotels.

CHAPTER III

WHO OWNS HOTELS, AND MOTELS, AND WHY?

The why is easy to determine, if not so easy to understand. One would think that the motivation to own a hotel is to make money. That is not always the case however.

Excluding major chains, hostelries are too often built or bought due to ego. This is sometimes true of companies and often true of individuals. There is something sexy and prestigious about owning a hotel. Far more so than owning rental houses, shopping centers, and office buildings. Why is this so? I have no idea. I am sure there are many exceptions, but I have never met a successful real estate developer who didn't lust for a hotel in his portfolio of properties.

One of the hotels that I managed was bought out of bankruptcy by a wealthy lawyer. His stated motive was to avoid having a major derelict building in the middle of the city. This man owned professional sports teams, a racehorse, a twenty-story office building, several other pieces of real estate, and lord knows what else.

He came to the hotel every day to have lunch with me. He agonized over whether there was a light bulb out under the marquee or if a cigarette butt was in the gutter outside the front door. He later told me that buying a hotel was the dumbest mistake he had ever made.

We once built and managed a property for a timber company. At one point, (over one of my too few two-martini lunches,) I asked the CEO of the company why a logging company wanted to own a hotel. His answer said it all. He said, "We are bored with raising and logging timber and making paper. It really isn't very exciting or sexy, you know. Now, a hotel is another matter." I agreed that a hotel was certainly different from growing and cutting trees and started on my second martini.

Is owning a hotel sexy? I owned two and I never found anything sexy about it. But, maybe that was because I was embroiled in the day-to-day business of running them. Is *owning* a hotel as exciting as that CEO envisioned it? Not really, but it is exciting to *manage* one.

I once went to a hotel I was managing at 3 a.m., (which I often did, to see what was going on in the middle of the night,) and found that the night auditor was not at the desk. The night cleaner told me that the auditor was out on the ledge on the sixth floor. I got a key to a vacant room and looked out the window. Sure enough, the auditor was on his hands and knees looking in a window. I told him to get the hell off the ledge. When he climbed back into the room, I asked him what he was doing out there. He said that he was sure the couple in the room was not married, and if they were having sex, he intended to call the police. I fired him on the spot and finished the night audit myself.

In that particular city, it was against the law to occupy a hotel room with any adult who was not married to you, or was not your natural born daughter or son. In other cities and states, there are unique laws too. In one, it is against the law for a female to sit at a bar unescorted. In another, a woman cannot move her drink from one table to another. Her escort or a waiter must move the glass.

Most commonly, people think that the corporate chain with the sign out front-Hilton, Sheraton, Holiday Inn, and so on-owns the hotel. Not true. Neither do the chains manage most of them. True, these corporations do own and manage some of them, but that is the exception rather than the rule. The vast majority of named hotels are franchises. For those of you who are not aware of what a franchise is, I'll give you the basics. The franchise company rents the rights to use their corporate chain name, such as Sheraton to the proprietor for a fee. They charge an upfront fee, put their sign out front, and use their chain name on all printed material and advertising. They also charge a fee based on room revenue, and put your hotel into their reservation system. With that franchise, there are also certain requirements about the condition of your hotel and some service standards.

So then, who does own hotels?

The ownership of hotel real estate is as varied as the properties themselves. How these owners came to own hotels varies widely as their objectives in owning them.

Some of the owners I have worked for have included the following, in addition to the lawyer and the timber company.

Large insurance companies, banks, savings and loan companies, brokerage firms, and credit unions often own hotels. Real Estate Investment Trusts (REITs) are among those with hotels, too. These lenders generally take ownership due to a company foreclosing on a mortgage. However, we built one from the ground up for an insurance company, which decided it would be a good way to invest its surplus cash. One dedicated REIT currently buys hotels.

Where ownership is taken via foreclosure, the stated objective of the lender is to renovate the property as needed, grow sales, improve profit, and sell it as quickly as possible. That is very straightforward. These owners almost never try to run the property themselves. They generally hire a professional management company that specializes in running hotels. We actually took over the management of an entire chain of hotels that went into the tank, with a brokerage firm taking ownership.

The developer or other individual owner is on an ego trip, more often than not. He wants to drive by with his friends and point to his hotel. He wants to take them there for dinner. He doesn't even expect it to make a lot of money. He just wants to be proud of the hotel and not have it suck him into bankruptcy. He also likes the huge tax write-offs. As long as he hears compliments about the hotel and he doesn't have to write six-digit checks every year to sustain it, he is happy.

It is not too unusual that the developer or individual owner views his hotel as his personal playground for his free evenings. We took one such property, where we fired a department head the first day. The developer objected and demanded that we re-hire her. I refused. The next day his wife came and thanked me for breaking up his little love nest. We declined to manage one hotel because the owner said that one of the busboys was in effect, a "sacred cow." The owner also permitted that busboy to go to the owner's suite when not on duty in the restaurant.

You may ask why a university would own a hotel. They view a hotel as a status symbol for their campus, and a convenience. Universities with hotel management programs have on-campus hotels where they teach many of their hotel education courses, and where students can "practice." Even if the hotel operates at a loss, it will probably cost them less than their sports programs. Historically, they would just go to the state legislature for more money or raise the tuition to cover losses. It isn't that simple anymore.

What is a hospital doing in the hotel business? A hotel attached to a large hospital provides a major convenience for the family and friends of hospital patients. That way, they have a built in market.

A charity? Yes, these properties are usually donated for tax reasons. The charity, having certain tax advantages, can often use a hotel as a source of income, where before, when assessed with heavy taxes, the property was not profitable.

We even managed a training facility for a youth group.

Mega-companies sometimes buy hotels and convert them into corporate training centers. These companies are not concerned about the property making money. Why should they be? They are the only client, so why charge themselves more to show a profit in their hotel.

Individual investors and investment groups as owners are some of the hardest to deal with for a management company and the hotel manager. These are often organized as limited partnerships, with the general partner required to fund all operating losses, and get the lion's share of operating profits. He wants the hotel to make money. The limited partners are in the deal for tax write-offs and do not want profits. This diversity of objectives is a considerable stress point between partners and management.

In one of the resorts that we managed with this type of owner-ship structure, the typical problem erupted. We improved the hotel profits by $500,000 in the first year, taking it from a lot of red ink to a profit. I got a call from one of the limited partners, telling me that he was very unhappy with this turn of events. After getting him calmed down, he actually hired our company to show him how he could make money in a hotel where he was the sole owner.

Some of these investment groups are professional associations such as a group of lawyers or doctors. At the risk of upsetting such professionals, I will say here that they usually have no busi-ness owning a hotel. They tend to be what I refer to as "focused geniuses." They may be great brain surgeons or superstars in front of a jury, but they generally have zero business sense when it comes to owning a hotel. To make matters worse, they each have a tendency to pop into the hotel on a regular basis to give countermanding instructions to the hotel manager.

One property we managed had an owner who wanted to call all the shots. He insisted that the way to grow sales was to fire the sales director and rent billboards. The billboards were to feature a banner proclaiming that there were sixty-four items in the vending machine. Now, that would certainly make one want to zip in and spend a night or two.

For a few months, I managed a hotel owned by five doctors. One insisted that I buy our meat from a specific retail meat market, owned by a friend of his. Our quality went to Hell, our food costs went up, and so did guest complaints. In a few days, another of the good doctors came in and fired my chef because the steaks were bad. That capped it, and I quit.

A property owned by a group of family members is usually a disaster. Family members seldom agree on long-term ways to handle their investment. Some want to renovate, some want to sell, some want tax write offs, some want cash flow, one wants to fire the manager and run it himself, and so on.

Construction companies have occasionally built hotels to create a market for their surplus materials and labor. Usually these are located on inexpensive land with difficult access issues and are ill-conceived projects.

Development companies will often add a hotel to their "mixed use" development. These usually include some resort amenities, home sites, and sometimes a condominium building. Their objective is to build it fast, at the least cost, sell the home sites and condominium units, and then get out of town. Construction quality is often poor and site considerations are often not compatible for housing, and hotels. In three of these developments, we wound up not just running the hotel and resort amenities, but also managing the homeowners association. In two of them, we managed the time-share operation, too.

One such mixed-use development had a ten-story hotel. There was one room on each floor. I don't know who had that idea, but they should have been hung from the tenth floor balcony.

One of the lesser-known and most unusual hotel owners I've encountered was an Indian tribe. They figured that since they were into the gaming business, they should add a hotel to the complex. That would allow their gamblers to stay and gamble for several days. It made for a unique set of problems for management, because the tribe was an independent nation and didn't always abide by the laws of our land.

Some resorts have incremental ownership, or what is commonly called time-sharing in one wing of the building. That means that there many owners, all whom know more about running a hotel than the management. At least *they* think so.

Another complicated situation occurs when a resort has different ownership for different parts of the facility. One entity might own the hotel building, another entity owns the golf course, a third owns the marina, and so forth. Obviously, these diverse owners have widely varying objectives, which makes management of the group very lively.

Now, having waded through to this point, you have a basic understanding of what a hotel is and who your boss is likely to be, and a very vague hint at what can happen in hotels.

CHAPTER IV

Who Manages Hotels?

That is an easy answer, the manager, right? Not so fast-it isn't that clear cut and simple.

As stated earlier, most of the major hotel chains manage some, but not all of the hotels flying their banner. In fact, they manage a very small percentage of their name-brand hotels; the majority of these are franchised.

The franchising company thinks they can tell the manager how to manage. Some wanted to dictate price strategy. For example, Hilton Hotels used to mandate that a hotel have five rate levels. Now that may make a lot of sense if your hotel has rooms of various sizes and views. Ten percent of the rooms were to be in the bottom and top rates categories, and twenty percent in the next to bottom and top, with the remaining forty percent in the middle. The theory was that you should average the middle rate. However, I had one Hilton that had rooms of all the same size, decor, view, etc. So creating five rate-classes became very arbitrary. Repeat guests soon figured that out and always took the bottom rate. The franchise company will also want a hand in the layout of all printed material and advertising, when to renovate the facilities, and the service levels. Of course, that makes sense from their point of view. They have a real need to maintain a certain standard for their chain of properties. However, those dictates do not always mesh with the ownership objectives or the economic realities of the property.

The owner(s) often want to play a major role in some or all issues. Many of the smaller hotels/motels with local ownership will hire a general manager to handle all the routine duties of hiring, training, and all the other daily chores, but the actual property owner retains all major management decisions. These include not just capital investment issues, but room rates, menu items and pricing, advertising, etc.

We took management control of one hotel when the owner's manager couldn't make the property profitable. The owner insisted that we keep a particular brand of canned boiled potatoes available, since her best friend loved them. I refused to serve canned boiled potatoes of any brand. The next problem was when she demanded that we hire her friend's son as a cook. (He was a seventeen-year-old high school dropout with a drug problem.) We canceled our contract when she objected to my assigning a black manager to the hotel. She had the audacity to tell me that she had nothing against blacks, her family had used them as house servants her whole life, but she wouldn't have one managing her hotel.

However, in view of what I said in the last chapter about the variety of owners and their varied objectives, it is reasonable to say that a very large number of hotels and resorts, including larger motels, have management companies running them. The management company may also have a minor ownership position in the hotel. These are companies that specialize in managing hotels and that might become the employer of all those who work at the location. Most management companies are fairly small and regional. However, a handful of very large ones are national or even international in scope. These kinds of companies probably offer the best career opportunities for a person who hopes to make a life in hotel management. The larger management companies offer a wide variety of experiences, significant support and training, and career advancement.

So having said all that, let's look at the management structure within a medium-size full service hotel or resort. The guy at the pool with his wife will need to know this. To keep it simple, we will use a 300-room hotel with a coffee shop, an upscale restaurant, one bar, a pool, a ballroom that seats 400, and six smaller meeting rooms. While situations will vary, this structure would be typical.

At the top of the local heap is a general manager (GM). He or she reports to the owner or to someone on the corporate level, probably a regional manager.

Under the GM, there will be a resident manager or assistant manager. In effect, this is the number two in authority and usually the rooms department's manager, as well. The unit managers will be the executive housekeeper and the front office manager, a bell captain, the head of security, and perhaps a reservation manager.

There will be a food and beverage manager (F&B, a department head). The executive chef, the chief steward, the bar manager, the catering manager, the purchasing agent, the coffee shop manager, and the restaurant manager all report to the F&B manager (those are all unit managers). All food and beverage employees report to the unit managers.

Another with department head status is the marketing manager. This person will have one or more sales people, and they will interface with any outside advertising and public relations people. Their responsibility is to keep the hotel rooms as full as possible, mostly by booking company meetings, and small regional conventions.

The chief engineer is a department head and is responsible for all maintenance.

The personnel or human resources manager rounds out the list of department heads, all reporting to the GM.

This is the basic structure of the management team at the local level. Many hotels have a program called the "Manager on Duty." On a rotating schedule, one of the department heads will be on call as a first response manager. This not only eases the burden on the GM and the Resident Manager, but also provides good training for the department heads outside their area of expertise.

A side note is in order here. Some chains have opted to go to a segmented structure, where most of the department heads work for someone at the corporate level, and the GM of the hotel has limited control over these people. I worked for one chain, which tried that structure and it was a total disaster. My personal opinion is that you cannot hold a manager responsible if he or she doesn't have the authority to manage.

So how does one get to the top of the pile?

Well, there are three ways.

The first method is to have a rich daddy. Not recommended. If your rich daddy wants to build a hotel for you to manage, I suggest you instead become a doctor, lawyer, or Indian Chief. We had one such hotel that we opened and operated. As the hotel stabilized, the rich daddy said that he wanted to put his son in to manage the hotel. It failed in six months.

The second option is to go to a college or university and get a degree. Many chains and large management companies look to these graduates for new budding talent. However, don't expect or accept a job as general manager right out of school. You are not ready yet, even though most graduates think they are. Look for a position as a management trainee, or as a department head and work your way up as you gain experience.

Then there is the most common way. That is to get a job in a hotel as a desk clerk, waitress, sales representative, or some other line position. Work hard, get experience in all departments, listen, learn from everyone, and keep your nose clean. You will be promoted, since there is an extreme need for good management talent in the industry. Just be careful that you are not one who is promoted to your level of incompetence, which is all too common.

Fortunately, not everyone wants to be a manager. There are great opportunities in the industry for people other than the guy or gal sitting on the top of the management pyramid. For example, the executive chef in a hotel may easily make over $75,000 per year, perhaps more than the GM makes. If you love to cook and this is your goal, get a culinary degree instead of a hotel management degree. The director of marketing is also well paid, as is the F&B manager.

I am always amazed and a bit shocked at how little most people know about hotels. In Iowa, I had a young lady apply for a job. She was cute, blond, blue eyed, and fresh off the farm. When asked what type of job she was looking for she boldly told me that she wanted to be a call girl. Now, since I was young myself (twenty-five) and had grown up in a small mid-western town, I was a bit naive. I assumed this girl wanted to work on the switchboard. Not so-she really did want to be a call girl. I finally got that message when she began opening her blouse to offer a sample of her talents, which I respectfully declined. Her theory was that when a male guest wanted company for the evening, I could call her and she would give me ten percent of her fee. (I could take my cut in cash or trade!) I explained that neither the hotel nor I hired call girls, or contracted with same, and suggested she button her blouse and go to college.

Allow me to say a few words here about call girls, more commonly known as prostitutes. They can be the scourge of a downtown hotel. You can't keep them out. What you can and must do is to keep them from soliciting tricks in your property. However, the reality is that if a guest brings one back to his hotel room, there is not much you can do about it.

(Of course, you can always follow the example of my night auditor if you are not afraid of high ledges.) You cannot demand to see a marriage certificate from every guest.

Put your morals aside and turn a blind eye. If you can't do that, consider getting a degree from a seminary. As a side note to this issue, I would tell you that I have known many prostitutes around the country (none intimately, however), and they all have told me that over half of their tricks do not want sex. These men just want a woman to talk to about their troubles, fears, and dreams. They need a woman who won't look down on them or laugh at them. It makes me wonder about the condition of some marriages. When I have asked these women why they chose that type of career, they mostly have said it was for the money. A high priced prostitute can make several hundred thousand dollars per year, tax-free. However, a few of these women told me they had a lot of fun, without the complications of long-term relationships.

Perhaps this would be a good place to tell you about another incident, which made my life as a manager "interesting." A hotel manager has a dual legal responsibility related to the hotel guests. These responsibilities are sometimes not very compatible. A case to prove the point happened in a NYC hotel some years ago (originally reported in the book *Keyhole*.) The responsibilities of the GM are first to keep the guests safe, and the second is to protect their privacy. Sounds okay at first glance, but look at this event.

A deaf couple checked in on their honeymoon. About 10 p.m., the front desk informed the manager that a guest had reported a horrible fight going on in a neighboring room and they feared someone was being beaten up or murdered. The manager called security and went to the room with his "E" key (an emergency key that will open any room) and a pair of bolt cutters for the chain. Knocking did not stop the groans, screams, and general mayhem that was issuing from the room. The manager and security officer went in expecting the worst. What they found was the couple actively engaged in what honeymooners are prone to do. Since the couple was deaf, they were not aware of the racket they were making. Fortunately for the hotel, the couple had a sense of humor and did not sue for invasion of privacy.

To summarize who manages hotels, I would say that the ethnicity, gender, size, or religion of the manager is not a factor. Anyone who has the talent, industry, and drive can manage a hotel.

How much will you make as a hotel manager? Well, salary ranges are all over the board. It depends on your experience and the size of the hotel to a large degree. A small simple motel may pay $20,000 to $25,000 per year. A large resort or city hotel can pay well into the six digits, with many perks. These perks commonly include an expense account for competitive shopping, writing off your lunch and dinner checks in the hotel, and free rooms for your visiting family if you can't house them at home or just don't like them. At one point, I got so used to signing my name to restaurant checks with the notation to charge it to A&G (Administrative and General), that I did it in someone else's restaurant once. The waiter chased me down in the street to get me to pay the bill. That was very embarrassing.

When entertaining my mother in one of our restaurants, I signed the check and we left. Not a sophisticated traveler, she cautioned me that if I didn't go back in and pay that bill, they would have me arrested.

One other perk, which is not as common as in prior years but probably still exists in some chain operated properties and some smaller motels, is "live in." This is a biggie if you can get it. It includes a suite in the hotel. Living in a smaller property, your suite might be nothing more than two connecting rooms with a small kitchenette. In a large hotel or resort, it is likely to be a luxurious suite of rooms. Living-in will more than just save rent or mortgage payments. You have no food bill, no utilities, no phone bill, plus the luxury of maid service, and room service. In a large hotel, you would have a staff of several hundred to act as valets, doormen, a personal barber, a masseuse, a chauffeur, etc. A live-in position has a major economic advantage, largely tax-free.

However, a word of warning here is in order. If you have children at home, I would not recommend living in a hotel. I did it, but I wouldn't want to do it again. In my first live-in, my wife and I and two preschool children lived on the tenth floor of a city hotel. There was no yard, no neighborhood children, no place to ride a bike, and so on. To compensate for this, I created a playground on the tenth floor roof. The roof had an eight-foot parapet wall, so they couldn't fall off. I made a sand box, and hung a swing from the framework of the large lit hotel sign. All went well until one day; I stepped out the front door for a breath of fresh air and saw a tennis ball bouncing down the street. That was odd enough, but it was bouncing thirty feet high. After pondering this for a moment, I went to the roof where I extracted a confession from my four-year-old; he had thrown the ball over the wall. I told him not to throw balls over the wall. Two weeks later, it was Clorox bottle half full of sand. Okay, my fault. Back to the roof where I expanded the prohibition about throwing things over the wall to include everything I could think of; including his little brother. They then graduated to tossing pebbles down the bathroom vent stacks, which tended to pop out without warning into a bathroom, hitting a random guest in the back of the head or the middle of the forehead.

As your kids get to school age, you may also find that the school bus won't pick them up, since they operate only in residential areas. My kids rode city buses, which was always a source of concern. You will also find that your 300 or so employees will try to spoil the devil out of them. If not stopped, it will turn them into rotten little rug rats.

One day, my five year old didn't get home from school on schedule. A call to the city bus company confirmed that he got off the bus, as usual, at the corner by the hotel. After two hours of our staff, and a bunch of police officers searching the neighborhood, we found him. He was sitting in the pit where five Japanese workers were installing a new escalator.

He was sharing the workers' lunch and jabbering away, my son in English, the workers in Japanese.

Perhaps the only good thing about raising kids in a hotel is that they are exposed to some of the finer things in life, like fine food. Once, my eight-year-old son sent a Veal Oscar back to the kitchen because the cook had failed to add capers.

Pets are also a problem when living-in; of course, most hotels prohibit dogs and cats now, but that was not the case in friendlier times. In the hotel with the private playground on the roof, I also had a dog. It loved to bark down the bathroom vent stacks to hear the echo. Guests did not feel amused by that. The dog had a mind of his own and resisted being retrained. I finally had to give him away.

In one hotel, I lived in as the resident manager, and the general manager lived in, as well. A "friend" of his gave him a wooly monkey as a joke. Now I grant you, that is not a normal household pet. However, this monkey took pet problems to a completely new level. First, he was a drunk. You couldn't set a glass of any alcoholic beverage down for a moment without him chugging it. Beer, wine, scotch, brandy, he did not discriminate. Moreover, since he was so small, he got completely trashed on a very small portion of alcohol. When the monkey was in his cups, no one was safe. He could land on your head with no warning from the drapery rod, or from the top of a chest. That was disconcerting enough, but while on your head, the monkey would start yanking wads of hair out of your head. The GM also had a large wooly dog that created horrid fights with the monkey. I received a call one night from one of the bartenders, who told me that he was quitting and that I could come run the bar myself. When I asked what his problem was, he informed me that he would not work with these giant rats in the bar. I went down and opened the indicated liquor cabinet, and found the monkey on his back, sucking on a bottle of brandy. I once had to coax the beast off the eighth floor ledge of the hotel. After many such incidents, I finally convinced the GM to give the damned monkey to the local zoo.

Another problem with living in a hotel is the perception of privacy. One manager's wife, when she thought she was safe from prying eyes, came out of her shower *au natural* and was greeted by the window washers standing on scaffolding outside her eighth floor window.

CHAPTER V

How Does One
Manage a Hotel?

You may think by now that you don't manage a hotel; it manages you. If that is your thought, I will tell you that you are half-right. The hotel doesn't manage you, but neither do you manage it. A hotel is a building. It takes very little management. It just sits there on its underpinnings and does nothing. This is a disillusionment shared by almost all owners and even the hotel's management team. It causes many bad judgment calls at all levels. It is even a misnomer to call the manager a "hotel manager."

What you manage is people. Owners, peers, employees, guests, contractors, suppliers, patrons, and invitees are what you manage. Tens of thousands of people, whatever group they fall into, come to the hotel to conduct certain activities inside that building. Thousands of people, each one with a unique personality, and motivation, and interest, and they are what you must manage. If you think about that, it might begin to sound nearly impossible. Well, it really isn't. I grant you that some of these people will test your skill, and a few will drive you to near distraction. But it can be done, mostly, most of the time.

So, how do you manage such a wide range of people who can range from Kings to dish washers and from young bright-eyed honeymooners to crotchety old rich guys? (One manager I knew tossed a vagrant into the street, because the guy was sleeping on one of the sofas in the lobby. The vagrant turned out to be a very rich and powerful man, and there was hell to pay later.)

I do not claim to be very good at very many things. I'm not a great cook and an even worse maintenance man. By now, if you haven't given this book to the aunt whom you can't stand, you may also be of the opinion that I am also not so good at writing. Nevertheless, there is one thing that I flatter myself in saying that I am reasonably good at, and that is managing people. You will find that developing that ability is a matter of survival to your career, sometimes even to your physical well-being.

A word of caution is in order here. There is a fine line between managing people and manipulating them. Managing people is simply getting them to do what you want them to do, the way you want them to do it, and when you want them to do it. It becomes manipulation when it is done for selfish or self-serving reasons, or when it takes on a vindictive or malicious overtone to the other person's disadvantage.

To manage people well, you must first master managing yourself. The first step in that process is to know yourself. This is hard and uncomfortable if you do it right. You have to be painfully honest. What are your prejudices? (Everyone has some.) What are your weaknesses, and even harder, what are your strengths? What turns you off? What rings your bell and gets you to act? How do you view yourself? How do other people see you? You must know yourself before you can know others well enough to manage them.

Don't be surprised if at some point in your career, your employer asks you to go to a shrink for a psychological evaluation. This doesn't imply that you have slipped into insanity.

I have been through the process three times. The first was when the chain decided to have all management go through the drill so that they could better map out career paths for their key management personnel. The second time was during a job interview process. The third time I set it up myself for the management staff of my hotel. This was very helpful in my managing the interfacing of the management personnel. These sessions can last from a few hours to several days. None of these analysts, or doctors ever told me anything I didn't already know. However, I was always surprised that they knew as much about me as they did. These longer sessions are grueling. They consist of such things as defining inkblot pictures, writing essays, and personal interviews. One of the most difficult was an assignment to write an essay. (Easy you say; I did that in school.) Well, this was different. I had to spend a minimum of four hours defining what would happen to the world economy if the earth moved 250,000 miles closer to the sun. I was videotaped to be sure that I actually spent four hours writing, not napping.

The second step in managing yourself so you can manage others is to accept the hard fact that all people are high maintenance, yes, even you. It doesn't matter who they are, or what relationship they have with you. Friends, neighbors, relatives, spouses, children, employees, and guests are all included. You must learn to control your emotions, and often to hide your feelings. You must present yourself in a way that fits the need. There are those who will say that this is being a hypocrite. Perhaps, nevertheless, you must get good at it if you are to manage people successfully. Who among us hasn't wanted to punch his neighbor in the nose when his dog takes a dump on your lawn and kills a spot of grass? Who hasn't wanted to kiss the cop when he gives the other guy a ticket instead of you? But we don't. So we all practice self control to a somewhat inconsistent degree. You must take it to the level of an art form.

You will make thousands of judgment calls in your career. By the law of averages and because you are not perfect, some of those calls will not be good ones. Lick your wounds and try not to make the same mistakes again. It is said that anyone who doesn't make mistakes is a person who doesn't do much. Well, you could also argue that not doing much can be its own mistake, I guess.

The third step in embracing self-management is patience. A non-critical problem will often solve itself if given some time. That is not a reason for procrastination. There is always a time to act. But, don't make a decision, until it needs to be made. Don't act until action is called for. It is not always as easy as it sounds. Making decisions prematurely means you are probably making them without all the facts that you could have later.

Now you have mastered yourself. Perhaps you have also accepted the fact that people are, without exception (yes, you too), self serving, narrow minded, inconsistent, emotional beings, and not always trustworthy, but somewhat pliable.

Now look at what motivates people. It's money, right? Not really. Money is a major motivator only when one doesn't have any, or perhaps doesn't have enough. However, let me make another point here about money. Money is far more effective as a motivator when given freely, instead of as a response to a request or demand. You get a lot more mileage out of giving a modest increase when they don't expect it, than a much larger amount when the employee is demanding it.

To put it another way, you have to find each person's "hot buttons." These are the emotional buttons, which motivate them. Find those buttons for each person you manage and you can get them to do almost anything. You just need to show the employee that doing what you want serves their purposes, too.

Therefore, if not money, then what *do* you use to motivate your staff? What are the options? I have found that motivators range from titles, to power, to calling them by name, to prestige, to a pat on the back, or just an unexpected smile. The most effective in many cases is personal recognition. Let me cite an example.

I managed one hotel where the owner insisted that the hotel give a turkey to each employee at Christmas. I thought it was a rather expensive memento, but he was the boss. I decided that if we had to do that, I would pass the birds out personally at the employee entrance to get the maximum impact. I heard comments like, "How am I going to get this damned turkey home on the bus? My hands are going to freeze and fall off holding this thing. My husband hates turkey. Oh God, not another turkey. We just had turkey at Thanksgiving and I already bought a ham for Christmas. We aren't even going to be home at Christmas and I can't fit this into my freezer." Well, those comments with a few four-letter words mixed in soon convinced me that giving out turkeys was perhaps not the panacea of employee motivation.

So I didn't do that again. Instead, I had my secretary buy 400 assorted birthday cards. The personnel department addressed them each month for those having birthdays. I personally signed them and we mailed them to the employee's home as their birth date approached. I had employees stop me in the lobby and call me in my suite. I had maids grab me and hug me in the halls. They all told the same story; that they had never had a manager give something personal to just them on their special day. It cost pennies compared to turkeys. What was even more important was it did what the frozen gobblers had failed to do; it greatly improved morale.

It all comes down to personal attention. We humans all crave it. We can't get enough of appreciation, thanks, or just smiles. It is confirmation that we are important to someone. You want to motivate people of any group? Give them something just for them, not a turkey like what you are giving to everyone else.

Don't let your personnel use the same comment to every guest. At the bank the other day the teller said, "Have a nice day, Mr.

Vincent." That didn't impress me because she said the same thing to the guy in front of me.

Teach the desk clerk to say things like, "Have a safe trip, Ms. C.; I hope your stay with us was pleasant, Mr. X; Thanks for staying with us; Mrs. V.; I trust you had a great dinner in the dining room last evening, Mr. B." Well, you get the idea. Try it out by giving a big smile to the checkout clerk at the grocery store, and watch his or her reaction.

Something else that I learned along the way is that people lead four distinctly different lives. Those lives are not always compatible. They live a private life of thoughts and ideas, unshared with anyone else, even their spouse. They live a personal life of family and close friends. They lead a public life with neighbors, the grocery clerk, and the waiter in a restaurant. They live a professional life at work. None of these lives are peaceful and harmonic. I believe most people live their entire existence in quiet desperation, at least part of the time. This will affect their attitudes and actions on the job and as your guest.

One other lesson that I learned about people is that they cannot stand silence. In my young days, I presented a project to the President of the company where I worked. It had taken four months to complete. He looked at the massive report and said nothing. I explained it. He still said nothing, so I explained it some more. By the time I left his office an hour later, he knew everything, down to what brand of underwear I bought. People will talk if you don't.

CHAPTER VI

WHAT IS MORE PERISHABLE THAN A RASPBERRY?

Anyone who has ever bought a pint of raspberries knows that they have a shelf life of two or three days, maybe. The rule with raspberries is to use them or lose them.

One of the biggest errors that hotel owners and managers make is to look at a hotel as a fixed piece of real estate. Sure, it is that from the standpoint of bulk, and taxes. Nevertheless, a hotel room is a perishable product with a twenty-four-hour life span. If you don't rent a room today, that revenue is lost forever. An airline seat is the same. You must manage the hotel as a perishable product. Airlines have gotten very good at that, hotels less so. Let us say it is 10 p.m. and you have three un-rented rooms left in your motel. A couple comes in and asks your rate and the clerk advises them that it is $79. They look at each other and grimace. The desk clerk should say, but I do have a recent cancellation at $59. They take it. Your clerk just saved $59 from going down the drain. Give him a pat on the back tomorrow.

A hotel room has a fixed overhead, whether it is occupied or empty. That empty room costs you a share of real estate taxes, debt service, basic utilities, fixed payroll, and so on. The variable costs for that empty room to be an occupied room is minimal. There is the cost of the maid, a bit of laundry, a bar of soap, and a bit of electricity, all of which is probably less than the fixed costs. In the above example, the empty room would cost you something like $19 and to occupy it would add perhaps another $8. Empty it costs you $19, but occupied at the reduced $59 rate, you have a profit of $32. Which do you prefer? The problem is that few managers empower the desk personnel to make that kind of a decision, so the couple walks out, and you lose. Of course, in addition to empowering the desk clerk, it is also helpful if you share a bit of your newfound skills in reading people.

While the hotel room is the most perishable of the inventory that you control; it is not the only perishable item. Obviously, all food items are perishable. Even canned goods and frozen foods have shelf lives. Far more than spoilage, food must be viewed as perishable from the standpoint of inventory shrinkage.

No, that does not mean that the one-pound head of lettuce you bought yesterday is going to shrink to twelve ounces. What is does mean is that it may completely disappear, along with a steak, a ham, and even a TV. These things do not disappear by magic, but by theft; in other words they perish or cease to exist in you inventory. The perishable room revenue decreases your sales. In this case, it increases your costs. Both are detrimental to the hotel's bottom line. So who steals all this stuff?

Well, let me say here that everyone is a potential thief and must be viewed as such. I ran a seminar once where an employee insisted that under no conditions would he steal from his employer (of course, I was his employer at the time). However when I asked if he would steal milk and a loaf of bread for his starving children with extended bellies, he had to say he would. Anyone under enough pressure and given the opportunity will steal. Of course, you can't treat people as thieves, but neither can you ignore the potential. So, who steals from a hotel? You name it.

Guests steal. Usually that is just a bar of soap or the pen and pad on the desk, and the hotel views this as part of the cost of servicing the room. It used to be ashtrays, towels, and terry bathrobes with the hotel logo. That is why most hotels don't logo such items anymore. Some hotels now put signs in their rooms to the effect that if you like the bathrobe, you can purchase one at the front desk. The implication is that we will sell one to you, but don't steal the one in your room. Some hotels are even less discreet, and post a sign saying that the maid inventories the room after checkout and the hotel will bill the guest for any missing items. A few hotels even offer purchase options for furniture and the TV. I once found a lady distracting the desk clerk at 3 a.m. while her husband manhandled the room's TV out the front door.

Employees steal, too. Not all of them, but more than you would want to believe. What are a few examples, you ask? In one of my restaurants, we had gold-rimmed charger plates. These plates cost the hotel $20 each. Employees would take them to a pawnshop down the street and sell them for $1. I would go down each week and buy them back for $1.50.

As recently as forty years ago, it was common practice for kitchen employees to have what was called "toting privileges," (the right to carry something.) This practice goes back to slave days, the civil war, and re-construction. In the Caribbean, it is still practiced today. Toting privileges consisted of the right to take any prepared but unused food home. Of course, that encouraged the over preparation of items so that there would be ample toting material at the end of the day. What was worse, it expanded to include hams, cases of sirloin steaks, and anything else that could be carried by three or fewer employees, including sheets, towels, and silver serving dishes and anything else that wasn't bolted down.

I took management of a large southern hotel in the late 1960s to find this practice in full swing. I gave all the kitchen employees a twenty percent raise and stopped the toting privileges. One third of the staff quit. What does that tell you?

In 1983 at 10 p.m., the owner of a Caribbean resort and I watched as two kitchen employees wrestled a leg of beef out the back door and into the trunk of a car. He refused to stop them. His argument was that their grandparents had been slaves on his grandfather's sugar plantation, and that was an inherited right and part of their wages. I said it would be better to give them a raise and not make them steal part of their income. His response was that they didn't consider it stealing, just collecting their pay. He also expressed his conviction that acknowledging what they were doing as being okay would damage their pride, because then they would consider it as charity. He completely lost me with that theory.

While his logic was more than a little flawed, he was partly right. Many of the employees that take hotel property don't consider it stealing. In one hotel with a very high loss rate of room linen, I ran twenty maids through a polygraph examination.

For those of you who have not enjoyed a polygraph, this is a machine, which monitors your pulse rate while you answer questions. Some routine questions are asked first such as name, and so on, to establish a baseline. Then other questions are asked and if the machine shows a variance from the baseline, it indicates a probable lie.

Several of the interviews went something like this:

Interviewer (after establishing the baseline): "Have you ever taken sheets home from the hotel?"

Maid: "Yes."

Interviewer: "Have you ever stolen hotel property?"

Maid: "No."

Interviewer: "Have you ever taken towels home from the hotel?"

Maid: "Yes."

Interviewer: "Have you ever stolen from the hotel?"

Maid: "No."

All answers followed the baseline. The employee clearly did not consider taking hotel property as stealing. Some know it is stealing, but figure the hotel has a lot of linen and a lot of money, so it doesn't matter.

The bar is a major source of shrinkage. Not only do bartenders like to give free drinks to their friends, but also some of them have taken theft to a very imaginative level. One way of doing this is to short pour. Let us say that you pour a single one and one-half ounce shot in a cocktail. The bartender short pours one ounce in four drinks and then he can pocket the fifth sale without it affecting your bar costs. Many bars have installed automatic dispensing systems to stop this problem. I had one bartender who got even more creative. He would smuggle a bottle of scotch into the hotel and sell his scotch. To stop that, I marked all bottles issued to the bar with a marking that only showed up under a black light. Then the man rigged an inner tube under his shirt and filled it with scotch. So all the scotch he sold was his and he kept the money.

I won't bore you with all the ways there are to catch employee theft. Besides, it would just tell dishonest employees how it is done. However, one common practice is to hire a spotter. This is a person trained to watch for such things in bars. A bartender is not likely to give his friend free drinks while you are standing around. However, he will do it with a spotter sitting at the bar, since he is unknown.

Employees also steal from guests. It is far too common for guests to leave cameras, laptops, and even cash in their hotel rooms. We had a rash of thefts in one hotel, and started leaving cash in some rooms. We dusted the cash with an invisible powder, which when brought into contact with human skin turned the skin blue. I fired five maids, a section inspector, and the executive housekeeper.

Vendors are a major problem. While most supply companies are honest, it doesn't mean all their employees are. It is common for a driver to skim a couple of steaks out of a case and sell them down the street. I once ordered forty pounds of beef tenderloins. I happened to be at the receiving dock when the delivery arrived. My receiving agent weighed the crate and it weighed forty pounds as was shown on the invoice. Unfortunately, he was weighing it in the crate, which meant I was paying $12 per pound for the crate and packing material, and was only getting thirty-five pounds of meat. The driver had taken five pounds of meat out before delivery.

In recent years, hotels have adopted electronic card keys for guest rooms, replacing the hard key system. The main reason for this is that the hotel can change the key to a room with each new guest. If you have a hotel that was built in 1928, can you imagine how many keys are in circulation for any given room? This doesn't even count the number of section keys and floor keys taken or sold by past employees.

CHAPTER VII

How do I Make My Hotel Profitable?

H otels can make a lot of money. Hotels can also lose a lot of money. A 300-room hotel can lose $600,000 per year or more (not including depreciation). At that rate, the owner has to write a check every month for $50,000 to keep the hotel afloat. Owners get very testy after a few months of having to do that. The usual fix is to fire the manager. As the manager, you do not find that fix very desirable, of course. Now, the owner has fired the manager and hired you to fix the problem. To avoid this unhappy turn of events coming down on you, you must do two things. First, you must increase revenue. Second, you must control costs. That probably doesn't sound like it is any different from any other business. It isn't, but it is a lot more complicated in a hotel than in many other types of business.

Let's look at the easiest part of this equation first. Well, at least it is the easiest to define, if not always the easiest to effect. It sounds simple to say that we will rent more rooms, sell more food and beverages, rent more meeting space, and raise our prices. So you hire a sales team to book corporate meetings, and use your rooms for the company's traveling executives. The sales team will book weddings, small conventions, and banquets. That is fine as far as it goes. However, there are restrictions. You are restricted in pricing by several factors. Of course, one factor is competition. If competing properties are renting their comparable rooms for $129/night, you are going to have a tough time getting $159. (Be careful not to meet with your competition and get into a price fixing mess.) The second issue is location. A comparable hotel in Chicago may be able to price their rooms at $290. You will not be able to do that in Omaha, Nebraska. Some cities and states also restrict room rates to no more than what you post in the room. Then you must look at the quality of your property. Are the rooms clean and in good condition; is the food good and well presented; is service at all points of guest-contact good? Then there is the question of the property's reputation.

How do you check your competition? Spend the night in his hotel and have dinner; preferably, before he knows that you are the jerk who is taking all his business. I have also found that you can go almost anywhere in any hotel if you carry a clip board, wear a suit, and act like you know what you are doing. If challenged, tell them you are a health inspector. Better yet, tell the competitor's employee that you are considering buying the hotel. That will send a wave of rumors through their staff, creating panic. Hotels have a grapevine that is second only to jungle drums. Half the staff will know about it before you can get out the door. You will also find several of them applying for jobs in your hotel over the next few days.

Did the prior manager cut service, hold back on renovation and maintenance? Have there been cases of lawsuits, food poisoning, and bankruptcy speculation? All of these issues affect your ability to increase sales. This goes even deeper when you try to apply fixes to all these matters. Let us look at just two of them.

Clean rooms do not mean did the maid vacuum and put clean

linens in the bath and on the bed. Oh no, it isn't that simple. A clean room means removing all traces of prior occupancy. That means no hair in the bathtub, no ring under the rim of the toilet bowl, and no dirty sock under the bed. You must look at a room from every vantage point that a guest may view it. That includes sitting in the bathtub and looking at the toilet bowl. Early in my career, I asked our Executive Housekeeper why the maids didn't seem to understand "clean." She took me to the home of one of our long-time maids. Then I understood. The maid knew we were coming, so she cleaned the house and made a pot of coffee. The maid lived in an apartment that was just one notch above subsistence. She had cleaned her apartment to her standards of clean, but it did not match the standards of clean for a hotel room. I learned that almost everything is a matter of perception.

Is the food good and well presented? That seems to be a simple question. Don't you wish it were so? This issue goes back to the beginning of food service efforts. What is on the menu? What are the portion sizes? Are the preparation standards and portions consistent? If the guest or the spouse of the guest makes a killer meatloaf, yours is not likely to measure up to that standard. It is usually best to feature menu items that most people do not make at home. Avoid hackneyed phrases like "home cooked." Who are you trying to fool? "Just like Grandma used to make," will also get poor results because it won't be like Grandma used to make.

At one property, I had a restaurant named "Cactus Charley's." We did a cartoon strip in the local paper featuring a character named Cactus Charley. It worked better than home cooked.

Standardize recipes. I once visited the kitchen of a cafeteria chain. Their recipes were all printed and posted above the workstations. As the cafeteria manager and I toured his kitchen, he stopped and asked a cook why he was adding cream to a large floor mixer of mashed potatoes. The cook said that his grandmother always did that. The manager said, "Then sell this batch of mashed potatoes to your grandmother, because it won't get served here."

Part of consistency in food service is the presentation. Take a picture of how you want the plate of food to look and post it. The plate should always look like that when it leaves the kitchen, no matter which cook is on duty. You will find too few restaurants, even high-end chain operations, where you get a dish that looks and tastes the same twice in a row. It too often depends on who is on duty, and what mood they are in that day.

Keep in mind that your guest eats first with his eyes, then with his nose, and lastly with his palate. The food must look appetizing, smell great, and taste like it came from Heaven.

Now that you have done all you can do to make your hotel marketable, let's look at the more complex issue of reducing costs.

Be creative. Most hotels have fewer than 28% of their overnight guests eating breakfast at the hotel. In one property, we put a small bakery at the entrance to the coffee shop, and near the elevators. Who can resist the smell of fresh baked muffins? Our breakfast usage jumped to seventy-nine percent of the overnight guests.

At first glance, one might say that we should have the maids clean more rooms per shift, reduce the number of waiters/waitresses, cut food portion sizes, and buy less expensive food products. Well, that is probably what that dopey manager before you did prior to the owner firing him/her. What that gets you is dirty rooms, poor service, and bad food; all of which will give your hotel a bad reputation and less repeat and new business.

The matter of reducing the hotel operating costs begins with defining expenses. There are four categories of expenses. One, not a cash flow item, is depreciation, which is the amount of investment in building, equipment, and furnishings the hotel can write off each year over the assumed life of the asset. Since it is not an immediate cash flow item, we will ignore it except to say that a hotel must have a reserve for the replacement of carpets, and other furnishings that wear out. In lieu of that, you had better have a deep-pockets owner, who can, and will write big checks to pay for maintaining the hotel.

The three expense groups that are of immediate concern in making your hotel profitable are:

I Fixed expenses
I Semi-variable expenses
I Variable expenses

Included in the grouping of fixed expenses are such items as real estate and personal property taxes, and debt service. These are items that the owner may be able to have some control over, but as the GM, you probably cannot. Re-negotiating the interest rate and challenging tax bills are normally ownership matters. However, keep in mind that debt service is a big item. It begins with how much it costs to build and equip a hotel and how much of that is paid in equity and how much is debt. Before your rich daddy begins to get excited about building a full-service hotel or motel for you to manage, you may want to advise him that he should expect that idea to cost $100,000 or more per hotel room, depending on land cost, and so on. A full-service 300-room hotel is likely to cost in the neighborhood of $30 million. If daddy finances eighty percent of that, at eight percent interest, his hotel needs to create a gross operating-profit of about $250,000 per year to service and retire the debt.

Even though you cannot control the financing issues relative to the hotel, you need to know the terms. The owner will expect you to live up to them. We started opening a series of hotels that were being developed and Industrial Revenue Bonds were used to finance them. When such bonds are issued, they can only be used for the particular project for which they are issued. When we found the owners moving bond money to another state to develop another hotel, we canceled our contract. Don't get caught up in doing something illegal. It will be hard, if not impossible for you to prove that you didn't know about it, and therefore be considered a party to it. One of these two owners moved to another country. The other, a bit less light on his feet, went to jail.

In one hotel that had become very successful, the owner suggested that I should buy it. His proposal was that I could give him $200,000 and pay the balance off from hotel profits. I didn't have that kind of money and expressed that to him. A few days later, a man came into my office with a briefcase full of money for the down payment. No documents, no interest rates, no payment schedule were expected. In doing some investigation, I learned the man was legal council to a mafia group. They wanted the hotel and me on the hook, so they could launder money through the hotel.

The grouping of semi-variable expenses include such items as property insurance, liability insurance, union contract terms, and employee benefits. These items can be shopped and/or negotiated to a degree.

The main area of expenses that you can control on a daily and hourly basis is the variable expense group. These include food costs, beverage costs, utilities, supplies, and labor costs. (Keep in mind that supplies include replacing china, glassware, linens, and so on, as well as paper goods, and cleaning supplies.)

So, let's take a closer look at food costs. We have already said that setting portion sizes and being consistent with these is essential. Assuring that you get what you are buying from food purveyors is also necessary. This is not just in quantity, but also quality. If you are paying for prime steaks, you need to be sure you are not getting choice quality. That obviously means that your purchasing/receiving agent, and your chef, and you all need to be able to tell the difference. (It is a sure bet that your guests will know the difference.) The same quality issues apply to fruits and vegetables. If you are buying "fancy" quality, then you should get that. Do can cuttings. You may ask, just what is a can cutting? Buying the least expensive #10 can of green beans is not necessarily the least expensive. There is a difference between cheap and inexpensive. A can cutting is opening a can of low cost green beans and a can of a known brand name. Look at color, texture, and taste of the contents. Then drain both cans and weigh the beans. That is what you will divide into portions for your guests. Even if the less costly can product looks and tastes good, the odds are that you will have less dry weight. Therefore, you will get fewer servings out of the can, and your cost per serving will be higher than with the premium brand.

Now, having written your menu, standardized your recipes, established the size of portions, and taken pictures of all the plated items, you need to cost out the menu so that you can price it. This is really just a math problem. You add the cost of a chicken breast, the cost of one portion of green beans, a baked potato, the garnish, (don't forget the sour cream and butter), and everything that goes into the salad, (including the dressing). Look at how much you spent for seasoning and cooking materials (like fat for the fryers). Divide your cost of spices (such as salt, pepper, rosemary, and so on,) by the number of covers (meals) you served in that month, and add that amount to your chicken dinner. You are now ready to establish the price on the menu. If you want a forty percent food cost, you simply multiply your cost by 2.5. You won't be able to price all entrées at the same mark-up. You must also consider your competition, and consider where guest resistance comes into play. Generally, you can price entrées that people do not make at home at a higher mark-up than those that your guest knows the price of. For example, you can mark a Veal Oscar up more than a hamburger or fried chicken.

Many restaurants, including most hotel restaurants, make the mistake of mispricing add-on items. A guest usually comes into your restaurant to order a meal. An add-on is often the difference between making and losing money in your restaurant. These are items such as appetizers, soups, upgraded salads, desserts, and wines. These items should be modestly priced to sell. If your guest knows that a given brand of wine costs $12 in the liquor store, he is going to be resistant to paying you $36 or more for it. However, he may pay $18. So, do you want a $6 profit or have that bottle of wine in your inventory for a long time? If a piece of chocolate cake cost you $2 and you charge your guest $8, you are probably going to toss most of the cake in the trashcan. In addition to pricing strategy, consider a bonus system for your service personnel. Pay them $1 for each bottle of wine they sell. Don't be so stingy; you will be surprised at how much that helps. From the server's point of view, it isn't just the increased earnings; it is that you gave it voluntarily. (Don't forget to cost out the entire banquet menus and bar drinks, too, including that cute little paper umbrella and the cherry.)

A word here about inventory control. There are two systems of inventory control; FIFO and LIFO. First-in first-out versus last-in, first-out. In times of volatile prices, you can manipulate your food costs on the short term by switching inventory control systems. However, a long period of LIFO will greatly increase your rate of spoilage. Keep your inventories to a minimum. Surplus inventory is expensive. However, too little inventory is a problem, too. If your staff failed to order toilet paper, don't expect to run down to your local Wall-Mart and ask for 8,000 rolls of TP. They are going to say, "Are you joshing me, or what?" What is worse is that some guest is going to call you to ask, "Why the devil isn't there any toilet tissue in my room?"

Control your freezers. Food has an eerie way of migrating into freezers. There the food sits until freezer burned and put into the dumpster. I know one very successful restaurateur who refuses to have a freezer in his kitchen. He said it leads to inferior products being served and an increased electric bill to keep things frozen until they are thrown out.

Now that we have a grip on food and beverage costs, let's look at that sky rocketing utility bill. In the good old days, a manager looked at his electric bill of $2,500, grimaced, and initialed it for payment. Now the bill for the same amount of usage is probably more like $6,000 to $10,000 and creates a serious need for a rum punch before processing. The only thing you can do about the rate is to be sure that your hotel is in the right rate category with the utility company. However, you *can* reduce the usage by intensive and consistent training of your staff. How do you know if the usage is what it should be based on the amount of business you are doing? You set up a par utility format. This is a very complex formula; based on equipment use rates, number of hours that equipment is in use, occupancy levels, food covers, meeting space use, and heating and cooling degree-days. Once established, this will tell you whether your training is holding utility-use to the right level.

Some hotels have put door activation systems into rooms that turn off, or reduce use in rooms when they are empty. Areas that use lighting all day and night, like hallways, can be changed to florescent fixtures. One of the biggest wastes of electricity is the bathroom light. Most guests leave this light on all night, with the bath door partly closed, to provide them with enough light to find the bathroom at night. Put in a night light.

The largest single cost of running a hotel is the payroll. Hotels are very labor intensive. You cannot control labor costs at the right level by guesswork. You must establish a staffing guide, a forecasting system, and a par payroll. A staffing guide is a method that defines how much wood a woodchuck can chuck in a given period. A simple example of this is a maid. If you want the maid to service sixteen rooms in an eight-hour shift and you pay maids

$8 per hour, your cost per room is $4. If you have 160 rooms occupied tonight, then your maid payroll tomorrow should be $640. (The housekeeper staffed her maids based on your forecast of occupancy for the night.) If it is more than that, your housekeeping department is over-staffed. If it is less than that, the department is understaffed, which means you probably don't have clean rooms. Either way, the Executive Housekeeper is probably due for a visit to your office. While she is there, you may want to look at her staffing of the laundry, housemen, night cleaners, and inspectors, too.

Now set up a staffing guide for all other departments. This guide will define labor needs for given amounts of volume in all areas of the hotel.

Different types of restaurants must be staffed differently. An upscale restaurant takes more service personnel than a coffee shop. There are more trips to the table with more courses, and more time needed to explain the menu and daily specials. Do you need a cashier and a host? How many busboys are needed for how many covers served? Do you sell enough wine to need a wine steward?

The type of menu being served will define the banquet service. Staffing a lunch for the Rotary Club is very different from a seven-course white glove dinner. How many supervisors or expediters do you need for that menu and that number of waiters? If you are serving a four-course dinner to 3,000 people, you will require between 125 and 188 waiters; depending on the kitchen location and on how crowded the ballroom is. They need more supervision than one banquet manager can give. Therefore, you need to add from ten to fifteen expediters to supervise and step in to help where service is bogging down.

How about the kitchen? How many covers can a cook handle with your coffee shop menu, how many for your fine dining restaurant? Will your banquet volume require a banquet chef,

and how many cooks will he require? Does your menu require a
Sous Chef for sauces, gravies, and soups? How many covers can
a dishwasher and pot washer handle? How big are your kitchens,
and how many night cleaners do you need to clean them?
Properties with multiple restaurants and large banquet facilities
may have several kitchens, perhaps even one only used for Kosher
Jewish banquets.

How many guests can a desk clerk check in or out without
getting long lines and disgruntled guests? How many guests can
a bellman handle on check in and check out? What is the pattern
of arrivals? Do you need to add a bellman for a four-hour shift
during heavy periods? Long waits to check in can bring a travel
worn guest to a boiling point. However, long delays at check out
can mean missed flights, missed business appointments, and
lawsuits. Many hotels now allow you to check out via your
television in the room.

What is the square footage of lobbies, elevators, ballrooms,
meeting rooms, hallways, public rest rooms, and restaurants?
How much square footage can a houseman vacuum in eight
hours, and how about carpet shampooing? Don't forget the exercise room and the costs of cleaning the equipment, and showers.
Oh, and while we are at it, we need to add parking lots, land-
scaping beds (which tend to collect cigarette butts), the beach,
the pool and the pool deck.

As to the system of forecasting occupancy, I'll skip over the
details of that in the interest of keeping this from getting too
technical. It does warrant saying however, that the forecast is
complicated by guests, who often don't do what they say they will
do. They don't always show up, and they don't always leave when
they say they will.

Well, you get the idea. Now we have established our forecasting
system, and our staffing guides that define the par payroll for any
given level of business in all areas of the hotel. So while we have

a two martini lunch at a nice restaurant down the street and on our expense account, we will have the personnel department compare the par payroll to the actual payroll in each department and then have a few department heads up to the office for a cup of coffee and a chat.

Now that we have payroll under control, we need to look into our supplies. Franchised properties generally have to buy certain things from the franchise company or from their recommended supplier. Room soap and other logo items fall into this group, but you will still have to decide on the brand and size of the bar of soap you wish to use. You also need to specify the quality of things like linens, toilet paper, cleaning supplies, china, glassware, tableware, and so on, and shop them regularly. Always buy high quality paper and linen items that touch the guests' skin (no matter which end of the guest the skin is on) such as face tissue, napkins, and toilet paper.

You also need to make some decisions about uniforms. Do the employees take them home or do you have locker rooms. Do you launder them or give the employees a laundering allowance?

Is all this getting too technical for you? Well, hang in there, it will get more entertaining soon.

In specifying all these things, keep in mind that you don't want to complicate you guests' lives. In one hotel that we opened, we had specified an upscale bar of soap that came in a clear cellophane wrapper. The owner of the hotel, staying as a guest for the grand opening, came to the lobby at 6 a.m. wrapped in a towel. He angrily told our Director of Marketing that we must change the soap, since it would not lather. She suggested he try taking it out of the wrapper.

One of the biggest hidden costs of payroll and the biggest source of guest complaints is employee turnover. It is not unusual for a hotel to have a turnover rate of sixty percent or higher. That means that if you have 200 employees, you will probably be replacing and training 120 of them every year. Good employee morale and working conditions can reduce the turnover, but it is always high. (No matter what your turn over rate is, you will settle into a core of good reliable employees. Treat them well.) Selecting the right person for a given job is one of the keys. Just because an applicant has prior experience does not mean he or she can hit the ground running. You will often find that it is harder to re-train an employee than to train one who has never had your offered job before.

In one hotel, I had horrid turnover in the pot washer position. Everyone I hired worked to the first payday and then went on a drunk. I hired a man with a learning disability. It took a bit of training, but he stayed for years. He took great pride in making a dirty pot shine. He was very proud that there was one thing in his life that he did better than anyone else. All I had to do was compliment him occasionally. However, he was upset and confused if someone moved a trashcan from its assigned place in "his kitchen."

When an employee quits, let him go. I have never had much success in talking an employee into staying. When I have managed to do so, it is usually a short-term fix.

Of course, a lot of this can go up in smoke if you have a union hotel. The union contract will likely set not only pay rates, but also many work rules. However, don't assume you are stuck with the contract. Contracts expire and have to be re-negotiated. Learn to be a tough negotiator. If you don't have that talent, or if you have no experience with unions, get a good labor lawyer.

Now we have a hotel that is running like a well-oiled machine, with happy employees, happy guests, and a happy owner because we send a check to him every month. Now we can finally do what we thought we could do and settle down in the office for a nice room-service lunch and a glass of fine wine. Yeah, right!

CHAPTER VIII

WHAT IS IT LIKE TO
MANAGE A HOTEL?

Now we get to the fun part.

I have perhaps given you the idea that it is all about sitting in the office, approving bills to be paid, writing staffing guides, and shopping for toilet cleaning brushes. I suppose every job has its share of drudgery that has to be done. But being a hotel manager is a life beyond that.

Managing a hotel is like riding a huge yo-yo that is constantly taking you from the depths of Hell to a cloud in heaven and back again. One day you are standing on a hot tar roof in August, watching paramedics extract a very ripe body from an exhaust vent. The next day, you have a maid grab you in the hall and give you a bear crushing hug while she tearfully thanks you for the only birthday card she got. One day you are looking at the mess made when a female guest put a 12-gauge shotgun under her chin and pulled the trigger. The next day you are having lunch with the King of Sweden.

One day you deliver a baby in one of your elevators and that night you find the body of a ten-year-old boy dead at the bottom of your pool.

If you have trouble handling emotional highs and lows, find another line of work.

The experiences of a hotel manager are varied, to say the least. Some of the following events that I have experienced are gory, some are pure delights, some are almost too bizarre to be believed by the uninitiated, and some are so strange that no one could make them up. These events all happened, but not all of them were in the same hotel.

When young and still learning a business that takes a lifetime to learn and is never mastered, I went into the male employee locker room one evening. There was a homeless person sleeping on the floor. Instead of calling security to deal with the problem, I took it upon myself to wake and remove him. Nudging him with my foot didn't work, so I tossed a glass of water in his face. Bad move. He got up swinging. By now, I was committed to defending myself. We fought all the way down the back hall to the lobby. I had finally gotten the best of him, and since I was in a highly exasperated emotional state, I tossed him through a plate glass window. My boss took some exception to this rowdy behavior by one of his executives.

Also when young, I took a call from the police one evening. It seems that my boss and his wife got into a fight in a bar, ripping the place to pieces and were tossed into the drunk tank. The police sergeant wanted to know if I wanted to leave them there or come down and post bail. I got them out of the slammer. In later months, I came to realize that this was not one of my better decisions. This manager turned out to be a real problem.

Another evening, the night auditor called to advise me that there was a naked man in the lobby, busting up furniture by administering judo chops to it. He said he had called the police, too. I arrived in the lobby in time to see this au natural man jump over the front desk, judo chop my night auditor, and begin working on the furniture in the back office. Recalling my experience some years past with the vagrant, and seeing what this guy was doing to our furniture gave me more than a little pause about getting into a fight with him. While I was considering my too few options, a canine officer came in the front door. He released his dog as our nude vaulted back over the desk. The dog got him by the shoulder in mid-air and promptly mangled it. The man was hauled off to the hospital under police guard, and I found a night cleaner to clean up the bloody mess in the lobby.

One of the large convention hotels I managed was going through a $10 million renovation. I had a German chef who spoke only limited English. The one phrase that he had perfected was, "Get your bloody ass down here." (He was not referring to my donkey either.) I was so summoned one day to find that the kitchen staff was in total hysterics. It seemed that one of the breakfast cooks had turned to the man beside him and demanded that he stop sleeping with his wife. The man refused, by saying that she was too good in bed. The first cook took a French knife and opened the guy up from his groin to his chin. When I arrived, the man's insides were sizzling away happily on the grill, and two bakery ladies were throwing up on the fresh-baked breakfast rolls.

The next time that chef summoned me was to show a very large front-end loader, which had fallen through the ceiling of the kitchen. It came to rest with its front tires on the hot stove on the cooking line. All open food had to be tossed, since it smelled like burned rubber.

Then one day, the chef gave me the, "Get your bloody ass down here," summons and all I could see when entering the kitchen was sixty very large white eyes belonging to thirty very startled employees in blackened uniforms and blackened faces. It seems that the vent stack from the kitchen went up to the roof, ten stories above the kitchen. The exhaust hood had not worked for many years. When the contractor installed the exhaust fan, he put it in upside down. When he turned it on, it blew years of accumulated dust, soot, and grease from ten floors, down into the kitchen, which must have been like the wind from Hell.

The chef and I finally parted company under the agreement that he would be calmer working in a more serene environment and I would appreciate not being told where to take my bloody ass.

The replacement chef lasted three days. The cops hauled him out in hand cuffs for child abuse.

In my experience, poisonous spiders don't hang out in hotel rooms very often. However, I found a guest in my office one morning, claiming a bite by one. I sent him to our hotel doctor and had my secretary file the required insurance claim. Some six weeks later, the marshal served papers to me showing that the man was suing the hotel for $5,000 for loss of consortium. Since I was not sure just what that was, I called the insurance company. They advised that the term referred to loss of one's sex life. In looking at our file, I learned that the man had been bitten on his right hand. The insurance adjuster and I got a good laugh when I suggested they find out just what this man did in his sexual life with his right hand that couldn't be done with his left hand. The pay-off came a few days later when I got a suit from his wife for $1,000. It always amused me that the loss of their sex life was worth so much more to him than to her.

My office windows were rattled one afternoon by a large explosion. I ran outside to find that three floors of the fire escape being installed were gone and there were body parts plastered all over five floors of the exterior of the main building. It seems that the welder's acetylene torch tank had exploded. It took all afternoon for the fire department to hose down the building and a funeral home to collect all the body pieces.

I got a call from a lady one morning, saying that her husband was stuck in one of the new elevators and that he had a heart condition and was very claustrophobic. She feared for his well being. I got the emergency key, but it did not fit the new elevator doors. When I couldn't get a response from anyone in the elevator, I broke out a fire ax and beat the door down. He had suffered a heart attack, but did survive.

This renovation project was, to say the least, stressful. We had gone through four renovation managers in two years. The fifth one I had to wrestle to the floor of the lobby and take away his handgun, while he was shooting out the bulbs in one of our new Hungarian chandeliers.

So it goes in a renovation project. If you are going to do a total renovation, consider closing the place.

Major conventions are always good for a few laughs and many bizarre incidents. First, we should explore what kinds of groups have conventions. Some are corporate conventions for their management personnel, or are to introduce new products or services. Occasionally these turn into the proverbial Christmas office party. For the most part, these are relatively calm events, so we will pass on to more interesting groups. Before getting into those, you need to understand that many people do not behave normally in hotels. They don't act the way they do at home, or in their neighbors' houses. In fact, they often don't even act rationally. When attending conventions, they are even less conservative. Political organizations, unions, charities, and educators have conventions, as do sports groups like bowlers, skaters, and musical groups. One of my fondest memories is of a convention of barbershop quartets. There was music everywhere. The convention of yodelers was a bit less entertaining. It does little to calm one's frazzled nerves to step out of an elevator and meet a man or woman yodeling in your face at the top of their lungs. In fact, if you belong to any organization, it probably has a convention.

When your hotel is hosting a major convention, all the management staff is on deck. The Marketing Director of one of our hotels came through the lobby late one evening to find the desk clerks all wearing fezzes and pouring drinks for a dozen well-oiled conventioneers. When she investigated this odd turn of events, one of the men told her that the bar was too crowded, but no one was at the front desk and the clerks had nothing to do. So the guests took some bottles from the bar to the desk, loaned the clerks their fezzes and set up their own little private bar. Of course, this was a little more than a gray area under the terms of our liquor license. In most locations, your liquor license will define certain areas of the hotel that are licensed. Be sure you include guest rooms, so that you can provide room service, the pool deck and all restaurants and banquet rooms.

In another case, some conventioneers decided they needed more room in the third floor hospitality suite. So, they tossed all the furniture out the sliding glass doors into the pool.

Social and service clubs have conventions. Rotary Club, Lions, Elks, Jaycees, Shriners, and similar organizations have regional, national, and international conventions. I have belonged to them all at one time or another. I was once the only Caucasian member of the IBPOEW, the black Elks organization. These groups are among the most interesting. When you manage a large hotel, you can expect to go two or three days and nights without seeing a bed, much less getting any time in one while playing host to a convention.

The state delegation of one of these conventions brought a crate of rattlesnakes and turned them loose in the lobby. Even though the snakes had been milked of their venom, it did not lessen the panic that ensued among the 300 or so people in the lobby. The same group stole a police motorcycle and hid it in our basement. They also took a VW bug; driver included, and stood it on its rear bumper in one of the elevators, which of course shut down due to overload. By the time we got the car out of the elevator, the driver failed to see any humor in the ordeal, besides he had wet pants.

One afternoon, I got off the elevator on the seventeenth floor to investigate a complaint about noise. I was promptly run over by two motorcycles drag racing down the hall.

Conventions are events lasting several days, and are attended by people with something in common, and sometimes include their spouses. These, are in theory, organized events. Some of the exciting days for a manager however, are not conventions. College Spring Break is one of those "unorganized" periods. At one hotel crammed with spring breakers, I had to disarm a nude youth who was on our roof, shooting at people on the beach. Only when the police had hauled him off did we find out that the gun was loaded with blanks.

It is surprisingly common to have a guest who has had too much to drink, finding himself in the hall in his underwear or less. We had one case where a man came out of his room in the buff to get his morning paper. The door closed behind him. He wound up at the front desk to get a key, clad only in his morning newspaper.

When one lives in a world this chaotic and unpredictable, one's sense of humor becomes a bit warped.

The chain we worked for transferred my boss at one hotel to another city. My staff and I decided to give him and his wife a grand banquet as a going away gesture. Our featured event of the evening was to bring one of his prior associates to town, put him in a coffin with champagne and three glasses and place the coffin on the table in front of our guests. Bizarre? Yes, but it made sense at the time. Well, the first problem was finding a casket. Funeral homes are not prone to lend them out, and I certainly did not intend to buy one. When I explained what I wanted, one funeral director told me, "Look we have a lot of going away parties, but we never get the box back." The mayor's office finally found one for me. It was a casket used for viewing before cremation. At this point, I couldn't be squeamish about how many dead bodies had been in it before.

Well, all went well until we got Pedro (not his real name) into town, showed him the coffin, and explained what we wanted him to do. He flat refused and said we would have to kill him to get him into that thing and close the lid. I was not to be deterred so easily at this point. So, we did the next best thing. After getting the better part of a fifth of Jack Daniels down him, we finally managed to stuff him in the box with the champagne and three glasses. The funeral dirge played, the pallbearers delivered the goods to the table, and I rapped on the lid. Pedro jumped up in the casket and promptly threw up all over the guest couple. The party ended on this note.

On another occasion, we had a very "active" convention that was almost entirely men. They even brought a flat bed truck of prostitutes to the hotel one evening. The next night I got a call from one of the doormen saying that he had a pig cornered between the inner and outer doors. Thinking he had one of the women from the truck, I told him to throw her out. He explained that it was a farm-type pig and wanted to know what to do with it. I collected three of the department heads who were as fried as I was and we managed to get the pig into a potato sack and tie the top. We thought it would be a good joke to take the pig to our boss's suite and turn it loose. This was not one of my best ideas to relieve tension in the ranks of the staff. We knocked on the door and when Mrs. X opened the door, we untied the sack and tossed the whole bundle into the suite. All hell broke loose. Their large dog had never seen a pig before, and the pig had just been manhandled in a closed sack, this was a combination that made for problems. Between the two of them, they managed to wreck the living room, rip down the drapes, dump the tray of hors d'oeuvres, eating most, and generally panicking both the inhabitants. Well, with some considerable confusion and effort, we managed to get the pig back into the sack and get out of the suite before my boss could collect his wits enough to fire us all.

As luck would have it, our problems were not yet over. It so happened that we had a gourmet writer from a major magazine staying in the hotel, doing research for a feature article on the hotel. Now, this man was blind and traveled with a Seeing Eye dog. You guessed it. When the elevator opened to receive us with our traumatized pig in a sack, those two got out of the elevator. The dog, having lived most of his life in the finest hotels in the country, had exquisite manners for a dog. He just sniffed at the sack and sat down. The man, sensitive to the dog, asked what the dog was sniffing at, and I said that it was a pig in a potato bag. After a lengthy pause, he asked for directions to the suite that we had just destroyed.

The next day over lunch, the writer kept saying, "I am sure that I have met you somewhere before." I kept saying that was unlikely.

He finally connected the dots, slammed his hand on the table, and said, "By God, you are the man with the pig." So, I had to tell him the story, which wound up in the feature article on the hotel.

Where did the pig come from, you ask? We learned later that one of the conventioneers had purchased it from a farmer friend, smuggled it into the hotel and put it in the bathtub of another convention attendee. That guy kicked it out into the hall and it eventually made its way to the front door via an elevator. Rational behavior?

What happened to the pig? I wanted to have a pig roast for the upcoming employee Fourth of July party, but my staff convinced me that the pig had been such a good sport that it wasn't proper. We gave it to a petting zoo.

In one hotel, we had a week long convention of funeral

directors. In one of the ballrooms, we had many of the latest
models of new caskets on display. After a couple of days and
nights of trying to keep several hundred well-oiled funeral
directors from doing damage to the hotel and each other, I was
wiped out. About 10 p.m. one evening, I went into the semi-dark
ballroom with the caskets. On a whim, I got in one and closed
the lid. Seemed like a good idea at the time, though for the life of
me I can't image why now. While I was in the casket, our banquet
manager, Willy, came into the room. As he was walking past "my"
casket to turn on more lights, I opened the lid and sat up. He
screamed and fainted. That little stunt got me a very nasty letter
from the union.

I had a very angry Senior Rabbi storm into my office one
afternoon. He was hosting a luncheon for 300 Rabbis. At the last
minute, the menu had been changed from green beans
almondine (our purchasing agent had not bought any almonds)
to green beans Virginia. The banquet cook had never made that
before, and being under the gun, added diced ham to the green
beans instead of peanuts. The angry Rabbi told me that I had just
sent 300 Rabbis to Hell for eating ham. I don't know whether
that is true of not, but if it is, they have my sincere apology.

You will see the best and the worst of human nature as a hotel
manager. In one property in the mid-west plains, we had a serious
blizzard one winter. It came so fast and with such fury that those
working or shopping downtown couldn't even get home. They all
wound up at our hotel. We could sleep 420 people. Within two
hours, we had over 800 people who needed housing. We stripped
all the beds. Each guest got either a mattress or a box springs with
a sheet or a blanket. We had people in all the meeting rooms,
hallways and even the lobby. As you might suspect, some were
bitter complainers about the conditions. However, one out of
town couple with three children made it to our hotel from a
camping trip. He tied a rope to his waist so that he could find his

way back through the blizzard, and went to our garage across the street to get their five sleeping bags. We were snow bound for five days. On the last morning, the guests had a choice for breakfast of dry rye toast, prune juice, or dry bran flakes. We were out of milk, eggs, meat, and all other food goods. Our boilers ran on fuel oil. We were down to three hours of fuel when an oil truck made it to us.

Among our impromptu guests were a dentist and two dental hygienists. They delivered one baby and did their best to minister to several others who were sick.

So, now you have a hint of what it is like to manage a hotel.

CHAPTER IX

WHAT ABOUT LAWSUITS
AND UNIONS?

Lawsuits are one of the banes of a hotel manager. As you can imagine, some are slip and fall type suits, some of these are even legitimate. Of course, you carry liability insurance to cover these. The problem is that insurance companies are prone to make a settlement out of court, as they view that the lesser of the costs. But, they also increase your premiums every time they opt to settle a claim.

In our very lawsuit prone society, you will be sued often. In some cities, I was on a first name basis with the marshals who served the papers. I knew how many kids they had and how they were doing in school. It got to the point where I felt slighted if I didn't get a visit from a marshal for a month or more. I was sued 157 times in my career. I was on the witness stand so often that one lawyer said I was a lawyer's dream witness. I got very good at dodging questions, giving half answers, and putting a spin on my testimony that favored the hotel. I always stopped short of perjury though.

Of these 157 lawsuits, I filed one. I lost the case and filed an appeal. The appellate judge not only ruled in our favor, but had the earlier judge disbarred for taking a bribe from the defendant.

So what can you be sued for other, than broken bones in a fall, or an occasional spider bite? Well here are a few examples.

The first rule is never, never, never sign any document, or contract without using your title. To do so will make you personally liable. When someone is going to sue, they will sue everyone in sight. The entity that owns the hotel, all officers and owners of that entity, you as the manager, some members of your staff if they can find a link, and even the Mayor if he has lunch there often are all named. If you are going to be named in a suit-and you will be-the only way to avoid personal liability is to have used your title. That gets you covered under the hotel's liability policy.

Food poisoning is common. Like slips and falls, some of these are legitimate. A hotel where I worked once poisoned 300 teachers at a banquet. Three of them died, and eight others were hospitalized. During the course of the litigation, it came out that the refrigerated truck that delivered the turkeys to the hotel had broken down and the turkeys had thawed. By the time they got to the hotel, they were re-frozen. We didn't know. The court ruled that we had no way of knowing and were not at fault. However, just defending ourselves cost the insurance company over $20,000, so our premiums went up significantly.

While some seafood can be a high risk, poultry is the most common source of food poisoning. All it takes is for a cook to handle a raw chicken breast and then make a salad without washing his or her hands between the chores. Food not kept at the correct temperature is also a major problem. Follow this simple rule: "Hot food hot, cold food cold, if in doubt, throw it out!" Yes, it is costly to throw food in the dumpster, but it is much less expensive than a lawsuit. Even more costly than the legal fees and judgment, is the indefinable cost to the hotel's reputation.

Other suit subjects include:

Theft or vandalism of a guest's car is common. Theft from guest rooms also happens frequently. Thus, the signs you see in hotel rooms cautioning you not to leave valuables in the room. Some hotels, particularly resorts, often offer in-room safes. Breach of contract crops up, too.

Sexual misconduct or discrimination is hard to avoid. One ill-advised comment by one of your supervisors can get you into a legal entanglement.

I was once sued for sexual discrimination. The situation resulted from my not hiring a secretarial applicant. I interviewed ten or twelve applicants for the position, giving them all typing and shorthand tests. One applicant was a man. He came to the interview with pink lipstick, dangling earrings, eye shadow, and painted nails. He scored off the charts on the tests. I didn't hire him. Now, I had long ago stopped being concerned about what people do in their bedrooms, or even in one of mine. However, I couldn't see myself behind closed doors giving dictation to this guy with 400 employees speculating on what we may be doing in there. I barely got out of this situation without having to fire the lady I had hired, and having to employ this guy with back pay.

Marital problems can be an issue too, believe it or not. My Executive Housekeeper called one day to advise me that a couple had checked out, leaving a flimsy nightgown in the room. I had her send it to their home. I got a call in a few days from the man's wife, informing me that it was not hers. After their subsequent divorce, the husband sued me.

Another man sued me because he lost his job. My housekeeper sent the man's forgotten camera to his office. His boss got the package. The guest was not supposed to be in our city and the boss fired him. The guy considered that termination to be our fault.

The lesson here is, don't be a Good Samaritan. Don't return items to guests until they ask for them.

I was once sued by the husband of one of my maids, claiming that I endangered his wife in an unsafe work environment. This is the story.

Our hotel connected to the city civic center via an underground tunnel. A circus was playing at the civic center and many of the circus people were staying at our hotel.

The events, as is often the case, started out very blandly. I got a call from the front desk saying that a guest had reported that his cat was missing. Before I could dispatch staff to find the pussycat, the Executive Housekeeper called. She informed me that Maud, one of our most reliable maids, was in her office. She further reported that Maud had relieved her bowels and bladder in her uniform and was hysterically jabbering about a wild beast. I went to the fifteenth floor, where Maud had been assigned that day, and as I rounded the corner of the hall, I met the missing pussycat. It was an elderly male African lion. I later learned that he was named Jocko. (By the way, I had a brief tour with a circus in my youth as an assistant lion tamer, so I had some experience with big cats, but that is another story.) I walked up to Jocko and let him smell the back of my hand; took him by the mane, and led him to my office on the second floor. Upon walking into the outer office, my secretary promptly fainted and fell onto the floor. (Never hold your hand out, palm up. The cat will consider that a move of aggression and probably take it off at the wrist.)

With Jocko sitting calmly beside me, while I scratched his ears, I called the front office to have them send the guest with the missing cat to my office. As the story evolved, I learned that our guest was the lion tamer with the circus and that Jocko, being too old to perform, had become the man's personal pet. The guest had gone out of his room to find an ice machine, and left his door ajar. Anyone who has ever had a cat knows about their curiosity, so the cat opened the door and went down the hall in the opposite way from the guest. When Maud came out of a guest room to her maid's cart, she met Jocko sitting beside the cart yawning, with most of his teeth in view. She went nuts. What started out to be a simple missing pet issue, turned into a lawsuit. I also had a tough time convincing my secretary to stay employed with us.

So, now a few words about hotel unions and living with them.

The union has the legal right to try to organize your employees. If they can get enough interest cards signed by your employees you will be notified of an election date. Don't try to stop the union organization process. You will be in court for unfair labor practices before you can say boo, and you will have a union to boot. What you can do is prohibit the union organizers from soliciting employees on your property.

What I say here about unions is not meant to be legal advice. Get a good labor lawyer for that and get one at the first sign of union activity. What I have learned to appreciate is a lawyer, for any legal occasion that fights like a junkyard dog. (I once saw a sign in a yard that said, "Caution, bad dog." A few months later the sign read, "Caution, my dog has rabies." It finally read, "Caution, my dog has AIDS!") That is what you want on your side, but one who knows the law, when to back off, and when to tell you to do so.

So now the union has notified you that they have the required number of signatures and they have petitioned for an election. Now what? Manage the staff, as you should. Don't be a wimp. Don't roll over and play dead. You can and should discipline and even fire employees when justified. You cannot discipline an employee for signing a union card or for attending a union meeting. You can prohibit them from soliciting the support of other employees while on the hotel premises. Be fare and be consistent. Morale is very important in the outcome of an election, but good morale is dependent on good management practices.

The union will point out, at meetings they call for your employees to attend, every mistake you have made, and everything wrong with their working conditions. The union cannot promise to get specific raises or specific benefits. What they can do and will do, is promise to negotiate for better pay scales, better working conditions, better work rules, and better benefits. They can, and will show examples of union hotels with higher pay rates and better benefit plans.

Likewise, you cannot give new things to the employees during this period, nor make specific promises as to what you will do if the union is voted down. However, you can hold employee meetings to explain why you don't want a union, and why you do not believe the union is in the employee's best interest. Be aware though, that if you require attendance at these meetings, you will have to pay them for their time. If you do not require attendance, you will probably not reach the ones you most need to reach. There is little point in preaching to the choir, as they say. If a single employee approaches you regarding union questions, be careful. You cannot initiate the conversation, but if the employee does, you can answer their questions.

Document, document, document. Make notes of every conversation, meeting, and event about to time, date, how it came to be, names, subjects, and so on. You will need this documentation later. It may very well save your bacon.

In their petition for an election, the union will have listed certain categories of employees as being in their bargaining unit. These will include all line employees, and probably most of your lower level management staff. You can challenge that grouping. Usually, you can get mid-level management excluded, along with secretaries, sales personnel, clerical personnel, and any of your staff who handles money.

If you win the election, count your blessings. Continue to improve the morale and working conditions. Strengthen your position; the union will be back in a year. If you win by a narrow margin and don't have any unfair labor practice suits filed against you, then you probably didn't run a strong campaign.

If you lost the election by a wide margin, you probably need to negotiate the best deal you can get with the union. If you lost by a hair, you do have the option of "negotiating in good faith" for a year and petitioning for another election. This strategy is certain to get an unfair labor practice suit filed by the union, and you will only have a chance of winning next year if you see areas where you can improve morale.

In one hotel, I won a union election by one vote out of the more than 300 that were cast. The union filed over 100 unfair labor practice suits. We won them all. They were back in exactly twelve months to the day. Nevertheless, by now we had had enough time to make things better for the staff. We had even put in new locker rooms, and a new employee dining room. We won that election by a four to one margin.

Some years later, I took over a hotel that had lost an election ten months earlier. I didn't see how we could win the next one with just two months to fix the problems. My secretary called the union business agent to come to my office to negotiate a contract. When he walked into the office, he said, "Oh hell, not you again!" He was the same business agent that I had dealt with in the other hotel. Then he said, "Just write up a contract that is fair to all parties and I'll sign it." He stormed out slamming the door as he went.

Well, you lost the election and now you have the union business agent, and two or more of your employees, now union stewards, sitting across the table from you. Keep in mind that the union wants pretty much the same thing for the employees that you want. Better pay, better working conditions, and better benefits will all be in their draft contract.

Union demands have changed somewhat over the years. One demand that has largely gone away is cooks' beer. Yes, a cook had to be issued a cold beer every couple of hours. In kitchens as hot as hell, there was a need to keep cooks hydrated. Of course, cold water would have done the job, but the cooks wouldn't have been as happy all day. Air conditioning kitchens lessened the justification for that demand.

However, they want these things for different reasons than you do. You want all these things so you have more productive employees, and lower turnover. But you are hampered by the economics of bringing them to pass. The union wants them so they can prove to the employees that they made the right decision and that the union is their benefactor. They want to prove to unhappy employees that big bad management and ownership will now get their comeuppance. The union will want one other thing that they will never give up, this is the union dues check-off. You are required to withhold union dues from the employees' paychecks and remit the money to the union. That item is your main trading point in negotiations. Don't agree to it until you have milked every other concession out of the deal. The union knows by hard experience that if the employee is expected to pay the dues directly to the union, they will never collect most of the money, and that they will make many employees mad in trying to collect it. In turn, this will probably cause them to lose the contract in a year. In short, the union wants what is good for the employees to the extent that it is good for the union.

In some states, if a majority of the employees vote for a union, then *all* employees in the bargaining units must pay union dues, even if they don't join the union. Some states are "Right to Work" states and employees do not have to pay union dues unless they join the union.

You can live peacefully with a union. It depends on your being fair and evenhanded with your staff. In short, be a good manager. The union will test management from time to time, especially early on in the relationship. But, they will back off if you are right. The more times you prove to be right, the fewer times they will make issues.

I had always prided myself in being fair and applying rules to everyone evenly. That is, until one night when I found a group of banquet waiters and my night engineer shooting craps in a basement storeroom. I fired all the banquet waiters, but only put the night engineer on ninety-day probation. I wondered for months why I had done that. Then one night, I fired a restaurant waiter for drinking on duty. Later that evening, he called me out of the restaurant, demanding his pay. I explained that he could collect his pay the next day in the accounting office. He pulled a switchblade knife and began trying to carve me into steaks and rump roasts. Being drunk, he mostly carved air, but he did manage to give me one scar on my right hand. In the middle of this melee, the night engineer, who was built like Atlas, walked up behind the waiter, took him by the throat, disarmed him, and tossed him in the street like a sack of potatoes. Lesson: If you have a guardian angel, like I do, listen to him. Mine has saved me from major injury or death twenty-three times. He is a real mess by now.

Now, you probably know more about hotel legal problems and unions than you ever wanted to know. Therefore, we will move on.

Before some labor union lawyer sues me, let me point out that the above comments about unions, are my opinions. You can't sue someone for expressing their opinions in this country, at least not yet.

CHAPTER X

WHEN SHOULD I LEASE
INSTEAD OF BUY?

By now, your well-intentioned but ill-advised owner has put all the money he intended, plus some, into the hotel that you manage. The owner is either unable, or unwilling to write more checks, but you need to refurbish the hotel. Things wear out in hotels. (Here we go with "perishable" again.) The more business you do, the faster they wear out. Things also deteriorate just from age. In a salt air environment, anything metal has a short life. Televisions, carpets, bedding, computers, air conditioners, the asphalt in the parking lot, and a long list of other items need replacing or updating at some point. The competition will force it, the guests will demand it, and the franchise company will pull your franchise if you don't do it.

Therefore, here are your choices. One; you can convince the owner to dust off his checkbook and hope like hell that the check doesn't bounce. Two; you can convince the owner to re-finance the hotel, freeing some of the equity (if there is any), but increasing the debt service you have to provide each month. Three; and least desirable, is to let the hotel sink into a downward spiral that will ultimately end in a crash and burn, not to mention putting a major blight on your career as you steer your hotel into oblivion. On the other hand, there is number four and that is to lease, which will give you a lease payment to cover every month. Of course, these four options exclude the possibility that you had the foresight and profits to fund a reserve-for-replacement account, which is far too rare.

Now, let us assume that you need to replace 300 televisions, 100 through the wall air conditioners, 10,000 square yards of carpet in the halls, elevators and meeting rooms, and that you need to get the VW out of one of the potholes in the parking lot so you can resurface the whole thing. Oh, and don't forget that your two main competitors now have computer connections in all their guest rooms. (That creeping amenity beast rears its head again.) What you need is $220,000. So, over one of your all too seldom two martini lunches you present this, with all the attached documents for buying, shipping, and installing, to your owner. After the paramedics leave and the owner can again breathe on his own, he tells you to go see a shrink, because you must be bordering on insanity. He may also suggest you not put the shrink's bill on your expense account.

After many less dramatic meetings, you finally convince Mr. Owner to put up $20,000 for the parking lot and let you lease the balance of the improvements.

The next hurdle you find is that the leasing company requires a personal guarantee from the owner. In short, if the hotel doesn't keep up with the lease payments, they can sue the owner for the balance. He won't like that idea at all. (Our management company formed a leasing company to handle hotel leases without owner guarantees. We could do that because we had the hotel checkbook.)

Now you are going to have a lease payment of about $50,000 per year to cover, lucky you. It is very common for hotels to lease televisions, air conditioners, and kitchen equipment, things that on a worst-case basis can be repossessed by the leasing company.

However, we took one hotel where the prior owner had taken leasing to a completely new level. A bank foreclosed on a hotel when they found that the developer had skimmed their million dollar second mortgage. The bank turned it over to us. I found that the developer had not only skimmed the second mortgage, he had leased things that I didn't know could be leased. The usual big items were leased, in addition to wallpaper, paint, kitchen utensils, china, glassware, flatware, paper goods, linens, and practically everything else that goes into a major renovation. When I stopped making the lease payments the leasing company threatened to come repossess the goods. I told them if they could find a way to take the paint off the walls to go right ahead. We settled the more than $400,000 in leases for $27,000.

Personally, I don't like leases. But, sometimes it is the only way to keep a hotel competitive in its market. I don't like debt service either, though most hotels are heavily mortgaged. The exceptions are usually where a lender has foreclosed or where the owner is a large company. These owners still expect a return on their investment, but if you miss the mark in a given month or two, you are not getting nasty calls from the leasing company, the mortgage company, and the owner. You are just getting them from the owner.

If you are lucky enough to be managing a hotel with no leases and no debt service, go have a rum punch and thank your guardian angel.

CHAPTER XI

WHAT DANGER?

One might think at first blush that managing a hotel is much like managing a department store, except that you have a bar and pool at your disposal. You have probably lost that first impression by now.

Application forms for hotel management positions should come with a printed warning that taking this job could be dangerous to your health. We put warning labels on tobacco products, alcohol products, and aspirin bottles. And, have you ever read the warnings that come with your prescription drugs? You have to be more than a little desperate or slightly balmy to take them. The side-effects are often worse than the condition you are treating. They warn you of everything from getting ulcers, to sore throats, to constipation, to headaches, to joint pain, to your left ear falling off.

I once had a serious problem with vertigo. I got so dizzy that I had to hold on to a cane or furniture to walk. The doctor told me to lie on my back on the bed and hang my head off rotating it from side to side. I did that. If I hadn't been dizzy before, that would have done it. (His cure did not come with a warning that it would make you dizzy and sick at your stomach, too.) After an

MRI and a CAT scan, I finally went to a chiropractor who aligned my back and neck, and that did it.

We label everything today. When I bought a two-gallon bucket, I found it had a large warning sticker glued to the side saying that I should not let small children stick their heads into the bucket when it had water in it, since they could drown. Does someone really think that warning is needed?

An application for the position of hotel General Manager at the very least, should warn you that you could be run over by a motorcycle in the hall, bitten by a rattlesnake in the lobby, or attacked by an African lion in your office. Even with that, it falls short of the potential side effects of the job.

Before we explore those other potential side effects of the job, let me mention the volatility and potential danger of your chosen career.

You, as General Manager are to blame for whatever goes amiss in your hotel. As President Truman once said, "The buck stops here." Some of the most common reasons why managers are fired are: (Not listed by frequency)

1. You miss too many lease payments.
2. You don't make debt service.
3. Or, you don't do numbers one and two and you make the hotel successful. Then the owner sells it out from under you, with the new owner putting his daughter or mistress in to manage it.
4. You get into too many lawsuits and lose some.
5. You drink too many rum punches.
6. The management company you work for loses the management contract on your hotel and they don't have another place to put you.
7. Your spouse divorces you, and you go into a state of depression. (The divorce rate is very high for hotel managers.)

8. You fall prey to one of the many prostitutes you will meet, or a cute farm girl who wants a job as a call girl, just when the police pull a raid on your hotel, which makes the local news. (Get to know the police chief so you can be warned, or at least have bail money available.)
9. The stress finally gets to you and you have a nervous breakdown.
10. The stress finally gets to you and you start taking drugs. (These are readily available in hotels, due to the transient nature of your guests, and far too many of your employees.)

I have flushed plenty of drugs down toilets, but never used any. I figured that if I ever did it would all be over including the fat lady singing.

Even if you don't fall prey to those risks, you must be prepared to move frequently, often on short notice. This will result in having few close friends, being away from the roots of family, and so on and may very likely cause you to re-read number seven.

I offer the following incident as an example of domestic stress. I once worked for a major hotel chain for eight years and lived in nine places.

This is particularly tough if your spouse also has a career. Kids suffer, too. My boys attended three grade schools in three different cities in one year.

Hotel chains and management companies move managers around like pieces on a monopoly board. In one move, the moving van guys were finishing the last of the loading when I got a telegram from corporate headquarters saying, "Don't go. More later." I told the guys to put everything back in the house. They thought I was nuts, and so did my wife. Thirty days later, we loaded up again and went to a different city than the one we had previously packed for. See number seven again!

Now, I am not very superstitious, but I did finally find a pattern to this moving around. If you are in a position where you don't want to move right away, don't hang any pictures and leave one box packed.

When on my way to city hall one day, I noticed one of our desk clerks standing on the sidewalk crying. I stopped and learned that her car had broken down, her husband was out of town, and she had no money for a taxi to take her home. Being a Good Samaritan and seeing a chance to improve employee morale, I offered to take her home. She invited me in to meet her mother and her little girl. I politely accepted, the ladies showed off the cute little three-year-old and gave me a cup of coffee. What I had not realized was that as I picked up my employee, my wife was coming out of a nearby store, witnessed my picking up a pretty young lady on the street and going into her home with her . . . Revisit number seven.

I once knew a hotel manager who had been through so many expensive divorces that he said, "The next time I meet a woman that I like, I'm just going to buy her a house and save all the legal fees and stress."

When we took over the management of one hotel, I sent a team in to begin installing our control systems, and so on. They called on the second day to tell me that they couldn't understand why all the trashcans around the place had one or more full Ready Whip cans in them. I told them to search the manager's office and desk. They found a case of Ready Whip. He was sniffing the propellant out of the cans to stay high. See number ten.

A further word here about stress and losing your job. I feel that everyone who supervises employees should lose their job unexpectedly at least once. You need to understand what you do to a person's life and family when you have to fire him or her. I have fired over 2,000 people in my career, twenty-eight in one day alone. I never liked it, and neither will you. But, if you don't do it when it needs to be done, you will get the ax at some point for not doing it. I never fired an employee without losing sleep over it, no matter the cause of the termination. I have lost a lot of sleep.

A side issue here about firing people may be in order. If you find an employee stuffing his pockets with money from the cash register, you should fire him. For lesser infractions, you should give the employee a written warning and put a copy into his personnel file. This gives the employee a chance to correct the error of his ways. After two warnings and perhaps some re-training, if the situation isn't better, then fire the sucker. Most union contracts require this type of warning system, and it is just good management policy anyway. You should resist the temptation to fire an employee because your last wife or husband was blond and you don't like blonds any more.

Firing employees takes us back to the question of "What Danger?" Rule number one in protecting your legal situation as well as your body is to have a witness when you have to fire some-one. Of course, this isn't always possible, but you should try. Keep in mind that some employees won't react all that well when having their economic life shredded by you.

I once fired my secretary after several warnings about being rude to guests. She called me a rather unsavory name and promptly stood up and clobbered me with my desk lamp.

On another occasion, a banquet waiter purposely poured a pot of hot coffee in a guest's lap. I didn't inquire about to his reason for that action, but just took him into the kitchen and fired him. He followed me into a freight elevator with a table leg, which he repeatedly tried to apply to the side of my head. After some moments of our dancing around in the elevator, with each of us holding one end of the table leg, the door open and the F&B Manager gave me some much needed help. Of course, I was sued again in the bargain by the guest with coffee stained pants and burned unmentionables, which caused loss of consortium.

In one hotel, I ditched the security company and hired a police sergeant as our head of security. He staffed the department with off-duty police officers. One evening while going through the lobby during a major political rally, I noticed one of our three night engineers, somewhat in his cups, giving a Senator hell with some very profane language. I got the idiot-the employee, not the Senator-into the back hall near the employee entrance and fired him. He took a swing at me. I hit him and he fell backward, hitting his head on a corner of the freight elevator frame. The officer on duty at the back door yelled, "Oh, God," and called the sergeant who was working for the police department that night. With the employee out cold on the floor and bleeding from the back of his head as well as his nose, I talked to the sergeant. He told me to take the guy to the steep concrete stairs and throw him into the alley below.

I said, "Are you crazy, I'm already in trouble for assault and battery?"

He said, "Just do it." I stood the guy up at the head of the stairs, put my foot in his back, and propelled him into the alley (which did nothing to improve his condition). The sergeant drove up momentarily, called dispatch to report finding an injured drunk in the alley behind our hotel, and advised he was delivering him to the drunk tank. Whew, I dodged that bullet.

After hearing about the above events, my boss's wife gave me a wall plaque the next week for my thirty-second birthday. It had a picture of a cave man holding a very large club over his shoulder. The inscription read, "Yea, though I walk through the valley of death, I shall fear no evil, for I am the meanest son of a bitch in the valley." (A take off on Psalms 23)

When I took over the management of one large hotel, I found that the chief engineer wore a gun. He also maintained a single jail cell. Rumor was that he locked up males and whipped them for minor infractions. Females he usually raped. All were "people of color." I mulled this over for a few days and then asked him if

I could see his gun. While holding it pointed at his belly, I escorted him out of the hotel and into the arms of the police.

I'll spare you a full listing of these types of situations. But, there is one more that I feel compelled to share.

One night, at about 2 a.m., I found our Chief Steward sleeping in a storeroom. I fired him. At 8 a.m. on the following morning, the hotel owner was in my office reviewing carpet samples for the planned renovation of our Grand Ballroom. The office door burst open and two people shoved my secretary into the room. They, a man and woman, had nylon stockings over their heads and faces and each had a sawed off shotgun, he had a 12-gauge and she a .410. (It occurred to me that these two were probably not there to complain about bad service.) They tied the three of us with nylons and put us on the floor with carpet samples over our heads. After some minutes, they untied me and told me to call the controller. I was to tell him that the FBI was looking for counterfeit money and he should bring all the bills of $20 and higher to the office. While talking to the controller he asked to speak to Mr. X, the owner. In a fit of idiocy, I told him that Mr. X was "all tied up at the moment." That got me knocked in the head by the butt of a shotgun and re-tied.

While I was enjoying my unconscious state, the stupid controller, (who I had been looking to replace) came to the office with a Brinks bag of cash. When he looked into the outer office, he saw no one and all the phones were ringing. Thinking this odd, he took the money back to his office and called my Executive Assistant Manager to find out why no one was home in the executive offices.

Unlike the controller, she did not sit on her brain and called the police. By now, I had recovered, wiggled out of my ties, and crawled to the door leading to the outer office. Since I could hear no one, I decided to run in and jump them. Probably not the best plan, but the only one I had at that moment.

As I leaped through the door, two cops with drawn guns and my Executive Assistant confronted me. The fact that she called me by name is probably the only thing that saved me from being shot by the startled cops. On the floor were the two guns and two nylon stockings, but there were no people. When the owner saw the guns again, and that they were really loaded, he fainted as did my secretary. I had a moment's thought that maybe she had a circulatory problem, since she seemed prone to fainting.

As the story unfolded, it seems that a freight elevator around the corner from our offices had jammed on a gum wrapper, and it sounded an alarm, which the two bandits took to be a burglar alarm and fled. By now, my poor guardian angel looks like he was thrown off a speeding turnip truck. Fingerprints from the guns identified the two as a husband and wife hit team from Pittsburgh, and they were arrested as they got off a plane. They admitted that the FBI issue was a cover for killing me.

At 11:05 a.m., I got a call from my former Chief Steward, who we will call AH, telling me that he didn't know how I set off that alarm, but it wouldn't save me or my family. I called my wife of the time and told her to be out of the house in thirty minutes, get the kids from school, and be out of town headed to her parent's house in less than one hour, and not to come home until I called her. (See number seven, one more time.) A police check on AH (we kept fingerprints on file for all supervisors) showed that he was an escapee from a mental institution in another state. (My predecessor hired him without any background check.) He was also suspected as being the prime drug dealer in the area, but the police didn't have enough evidence yet to arrest him. The job at the hotel was his cover, and I had unwittingly blown it when I fired him.

I was given a concealed weapon permit, and I moved into the hotel with a cop in the adjoining room. He also took me to the police firing range for an hour every day. A few days later, the police picked up AH while coming into the hotel with a .45-automatic stuck into his belt. He was exported to the mental institution.

For the next three weeks, I stayed in the hotel and left the family cooling their heels in another city. Something just didn't feel right. AH was next collected near the hotel with a shotgun down his pants leg. He had escaped again. I got a court order to the effect that if AH escaped, or was released, the institution had to notify me within eight hours.

Several months later, I was notified that they were releasing AH because he was cured. When I inquired as to how they had come to that conclusion, I was told that he said he didn't want to kill me anymore. I asked the obvious question, that being, "Just what do you expect him to say if he wants out?" I couldn't stop the release, since they flooded the judge's desk with a stack of reports from his doctors saying he was okay now. The guy is still out there somewhere, and is probably still looking for me.

Of course, your employee manual will prohibit their bringing weapons to the hotel. But that doesn't keep the bad apples from doing so. Now you not only have to keep one eye out for some unknown number of your employees who are potential or practicing thieves, but the other eye cocked for some who may wish you physical harm.

Not all the people who would like to bash you are employees. Some are your guests, and it usually isn't over bad service.

I had two policemen pop into my office one day to tell me they were looking for an escapee from a state prison in a nearby state. They showed me his police record, which read like a dictionary of crimes and included murder, armed robbery, child abuse, and rape.

Armed with their list of aliases he used, I checked our guest register to find that he was in room 305. We went to the room and after using my trusty emergency key and bolt cutters, I inched the door open about three inches. The bad guy was in bed. The police suggested that I go in and wake him. I said, "Are you nuts? You have guns, I don't." They went in, and after a brief struggle; they subdued him to find the largest handgun I had ever seen under his pillow.

One year, we leased our main ballroom to a promoter for a gala New Years Eve party. The ballroom was fire rated to hold 1,500 people. He sold over 2,000 tickets. The first clue I had about the mounting problem was a call from the front desk telling me that there were at least 500 very angry people in the lobby and they were threatening to wreck the place. After calling the police, I went down to the lobby. A police captain I knew grabbed me and pushed me into an elevator, told me to turn it off and close the door, and not to come out until he came for me. As the door closed, I told him to find the promoter in the ballroom and put him in the car, too. When the sleazy promoter was ensconced with me, I told him he had to give the people their money back with a twenty percent bonus. He refused. I told him he was either going to do that, or I was going to beat him to a bloody pulp in the elevator. He did it, and the mob left.

One Christmas, our sales department booked a women's group for a banquet of 200 and an open bar. About 11 p.m., our banquet manager came to my office to tell me that she and all the banquet waitresses were walking off the job. When I inquired about the problem, she told me to go see for myself. That seemed a reasonable request, so I did. A woman who I think may have been a half-breed between an Amazon and a gorilla met me at the ballroom door. She refused my going in. With my curiosity now at a high level, I went to the kitchen and opened the door with my master key. I walked into a room with some 200 women in various states of undress or completely nude, doing all kinds of interesting things to each other. Upon seeing me, a large percentage of them started throwing bottles, glasses, profanity, and pieces of clothing at me. I retreated, locked the kitchen door, and called the police. I suggested they raid the joint, but asked them to keep it out of the papers. Now I am not a prude, but there are limits.

As in all lives, some things that start out peacefully can take a turn for the worse. We sometimes sponsored hot air balloon races to promote hotels. They got great TV and radio coverage. Sometimes they even made the front page of local papers. On one such occasion, I was in the lead balloon. We caught a down draft while descending to land. The bottom of the basket hung up on steel spikes on the top of a bridge that was under construction. The basket turned upside down, dumping the balloonist and me, along with several fuel tanks, out into a twenty-foot ravine. The balloonist got a broken arm and a broken collarbone. I got cuts and bruises, and a shredded $800 suit. My guardian angel got his feathers messed up again and a badly mangled halo.

While there are many things I could relate in this section, I'll stop with one final story.

My Bell Captain called me to the lobby late one night. He had investigated a lot of yelling in a section of the building that was closed for renovation and he thought I should come see the problem, since I probably wouldn't believe it if related by him. We went to the area and I had to admit that he was right. There was a very drunk man glued to the wall.

It seems he had been in our basement bar drinking, and had wandered into this section of the building looking for a men's room. When he went into the restroom, he had blundered into a large can of yellow mastic that was being used to glue down carpet and the lid popped off, allowing the mastic to ooze over the floor. When he came out, he stepped in this mess, fell, and wallowed around in it. He finally regained his feet and leaned against the wall. While dozing, the glue set. He was now firmly attached and was sure some muggers were holding him from behind. It became clear that the only way to get this guy off my wall was to cut his clothing off him, which we managed to do while getting a few bitten ears, bruises, and black eyes in the process. He fought as if a man possessed, since he thought he was being mugged.

We dressed him in an unclaimed suit and two mismatched shoes from lost and found. He looked like a poor relation of Bozo the clown with globs of yellow glue in his hair, his groin, and most other places. His wallet ID gave us his address and we sent him home in a cab. I would have given $50 to hear the discussion he had with his wife at 2 a.m.

CHAPTER XII

WHO ARE MY GUESTS AND WHAT ARE THEY DOING HERE?

This can best be answered by telling you who they are not and what they are not doing in your hotel.

Look around you. Anyone and everyone can be a past, present, or future guest in your hotel. They are all colors, sizes, shapes, vocations, and speak various languages. They come from all over the place, including their houses down the street from the hotel. Now it is easy to see why a person away from his hometown would stay in some kind of hotel. But, why would the person who lives a few blocks away do it? I have heard all kinds of reasons from, "Our house is being painted," to "It burned down," to "We have company that we can't stand." The one that I never heard, but know it is one of the reasons is, "This is my mistress, and my wife frowns on my taking her to our house." If that upsets your sensitivity, reconsider the seminary.

I once had my sales director come to me early one morning and ask permission to take a room in the hotel for a few days. I asked him why he would want to do that. He calmly, but slurring, explained that he had been out drinking the night before and had picked up a girl. They were both more than a bit tipsy, when he took her home to meet his wife at 3 a.m. She tossed them both out and followed that with most of his clothing. He needed a place to lay his head. I thought about that for a few minutes and fired him. No one that stupid should be representing our hotel.

We once took management of a motel as a favor for one of our clients. It was not a property that we would normally have taken. It was in a seedy neighborhood and therefore had a drive-up window for registration at night. That allowed the night clerk to keep the lobby locked and robbers outside. Our Director of Marketing (female) and our CFO (male) went to take control of the property. They arrived at the drive-up window at about 11 p.m. The clerk asked, "Do y'all want a room by the hour, or are you going to make a night of it?" Any guesses as to what the clientele was? That is a property that I call a "hot sheet" operation. I have seen some where every room had an enclosed garage. The reason for this is to keep your spouse from seeing your car at a local motel.

On my first visit to this property, I decided to go down to the soft drink machine and get something to drink at about 10 p.m. What I found were two very "butch" women working on the machine with a large screwdriver and a crowbar. When I asked what they thought they were doing, they said they were pretty sure they were extracting the cash box from the machine. They also informed me that they needed no help from me. I retreated to my room and drank tap water. There was no point in calling the police, since they seldom came into this district.

Your guests will include people from all walks of life. Every day men and women, with every day jobs and everyday problems will be your guests. They don't come to your hotel to get more problems, so try not to give them any. If they do have a problem in your hotel, listen to it, be understanding, and do what it takes to make it right. If the guest's steak was overdone, don't make him pay for it, even if he did eat it all. If the desk clerk was rude, then apologize for it and comp the guest's room or buy him dinner. The worst thing you can do is try to defend what happened, make excuses, or argue with an already unhappy guest. Is that expensive? Perhaps, but it is less expensive than having a person go away to tell others about his bad experience. It is said that a happy customer tells three people, an unhappy one tells ten. Remember, it is a lot cheaper to keep a customer than to find a replacement.

Most of your guests come and go in a routine flow without any problems and without blowing their brains out in your lobby. However, a certain percentage of them will be problems. Some just because they have had a bad day and are looking for someone to take it out on. After all, when a guy has been bumped from his flight, lost a big sale because of it, landed in Wichita while his luggage went to Chicago, and his kid flunked his math test, that prospective guest is probably not in a great humor by the time he gets to your hotel. With his short fuse, it won't take much of a spark to set him off.

Some of your guests are just professional asses or spoiled brats, or have such big egos that nothing makes them happy. Some are just a bit unhinged. Suck it up, manager. That is life.

My bell captain came to me one afternoon to report that there was an elderly lady in the ballroom playing the grand piano. The room was out of service for re-carpeting and was not a safe place for the public. I went to the ballroom and asked the lady if I could help her. She politely informed me that she was fine, and she was just playing the piano so her sister could dance. I scanned the room full of carpet rolls, but there was not a third party there. I went back to my office to think on this. When I returned to the ballroom, she was gone.

I learned from the front desk that the woman had checked in with her sister, but no one had seen the sister. The coffee shop manager said that the lady always ordered two meals, and ate some of both, but was always alone. I had the police run a check on her.

She was from a small town in Connecticut and both she and her sister were "old maids" and had always lived together. Her sister had died some months before and the woman now just traveled around the country. She was known to be more than a little wacko, but harmless. The only problem we had was that when she got on an elevator, all the others stopped running until she got out of her car. This odd woman turned up in my life two other times and in two other cities.

While managing a large hotel, a person who had held a prominent place in our national government some years earlier died, and the funeral was to be held in a suburb of our city. Dignitaries from all over the country and the world overran us. Governors, Senators, Kings, and all came for the event. As the manager of the largest hotel in the city, I had to play host to some of the most important. I had dinner with a lady from a royal family. She had the personality of a large toad. In trying to keep conversation from completely bogging down, I asked her what it was like to live in a palace. She said she didn't really know, since she had never lived anywhere else. When I asked how the flight to our country was, she responded that it was uneventful. So the evening went. I extracted myself as soon as I could do so gracefully and went to have a much-needed drink with a very tipsy Congressman. It was a step up, since the Congressman wasn't able to carry on much conversation anyway.

You will be privileged to attend many famous events in your city. These will include such things as the Kentucky Derby, the Indy 500, and political conventions. Events that under other circumstances you would never get to attend.

As I mentioned early on, you must learn to be a chameleon. Change to meet the situation. You must be able to calm an irate guest, then get up from your desk and have dinner with a Queen.

You will meet royalty and presidents. You will dine with famous sports figures and headline entertainers. You will rub elbows with many of the rich and famous in between being attacked, sued, negotiating union contracts, and ordering toilet paper. Those are your guests. Now what are they all doing in your hotel?

Well, you probably don't really want to know. If you can think of it, they are doing it. In fact, they are probably doing it even if you can't think of it. Again, the vast majority are just doing their thing. They are attending training meetings, they are having a glass of wine with dinner, and though hard to believe, they are sometimes just sleeping. They are on the phone making appointments and in the lobby catching a cab. That is all well and good, but sometimes they are not doing these things.

Sometimes you catch them having sex in your pool at 4 a.m. Sometimes they are trying to seduce your night maid, or exposing themselves to someone in an elevator. Sometimes they are either jumping out of your windows, or throwing your furniture out of them. Sometimes they are trying to steal one of your televisions, or rob the desk clerk at gunpoint. And, sometimes they are flushing a snake down a toilet. What, you say? (I know some of these stories are a little hard to swallow. But, sometimes life as a hotel manager is that way.)

I took security to a room one night when the night maid said she saw water running out from under a guest room door. Fearing a broken water line, I knocked on the door and was surprised when a guest opened it. He promptly complained to me that the toilet was clogged. We went into the bathroom to find the front three feet of an eight-foot boa constrictor sticking out of the bowl with another guest repeatedly flushing it. My security officer called the police, who arrested five guys for cruelty to animals, drug use, destruction of property, and many other things that I have since forgotten. It probably doesn't need to be said that the snake was very unhappy at the recent turn of events.

Animal control finally had to kill the bugger to get it out of the toilet. I know that this is one too much and you are saying. "I don't believe it." Well, it is true and if I told you who the five guest were, you would probably believe it. Of course, if I did tell you, I would likely be sued again. So you will just have to take my word for it.

One night, with the help of twenty policemen, I had to evict an entire professional sports team. For some odd reason they decided to have a water fight in the ninth floor hall with the emergency fire hoses. I wish they had just been asleep in some of our fine beds.

During the funeral mentioned above, we had a lot of press staying in the hotel. One of the TV reporters and his camera crew were setting up in the fifteenth floor hall to interview a VIP. Now this seventeen-floor tower had a central vacuum system. As you can imagine it required a vacuum machine that would take the hair off a cat. In the hustle of trying to get ready, the cameraman ran down the hall to plug in a one hundred-foot extension cord for his camera. He inadvertently plugged it into the vacuum outlet. It promptly took the extension cord, the camera cord, and smashed his camera into the wall. Fortunately, that activity is not a daily event.

Some guests come to your hotel to do themselves in. I don't know why they can't do it at home, or on the city bridge, but some of them don't. Standing in the lobby of a twenty-story interior atrium one morning, I heard what sounded like someone had dropped a watermelon. I turned around to find the splattered body of a man that had jumped off the nineteenth floor landing and at least twenty guests throwing up all over the new sofas. Suicides are always messy affairs. The most you can hope for is that they do it in their guest room and not in your lobby or restaurant.

After one of my managers had three suicides in one week, he

printed signs for the rooms saying, "If you are going to shoot yourself, please go home, or at the very least pay your bill first." I wouldn't let him put the signs in the rooms.

Sometimes people do things in hotels that they really didn't plan to do. One of those unscheduled activities is dying. I have had them die sitting on the toilet, in the bathtub, and on elevators. One was even found at 3 a.m., mummified in the hotel basement behind a central air conditioning unit.

One morning a maid found a guest dead and sitting on his toilet, completely nude. Rigor mortise had set in. The ambulance came, strapped him onto a stretcher, put a sheet over him, and took him down to the lobby. While going through the lobby with some 150 women in attendance, one of the straps came unbuckled and the cadaver sat up. That created mass panic in the lobby, taking a full hour to get the women under control.

By now, you may have the idea that I didn't sleep much. Well, I have fired many people. One night, the night Bell Captain woke me at 4 a.m., while I was asleep standing in the corner of an elevator. You eat and sleep where you can sometimes.

In one hotel, we had an unexpected rash of check-ins one Friday evening. Every guest seemed to arrive with a gun case as part of his luggage. I learned about this early the next day and headed to my office to call the chief of police to see if there was a shooting competition in the city, or was he expecting a localized revolt of some kind. Before I could make the call, I heard what sounded like World War III in progress. I soon learned that it was "starling season," whatever that was. Our hotel was the tallest building in downtown and all our guests were on the roof with their guns. I went up to find out what the devil was going on. Every roof in downtown was full of men blazing away with shotguns. It seems that when the starlings migrated, it was legal open season on them. People came from hundreds of miles around to shoot starlings. The sky was black with them, as were the streets and sidewalks. What few people there were out on the streets all had umbrellas, all of which were covered with bird droppings and bloody feathers. Well, when in Rome, so I got my shotgun and joined the party. More rational behavior!

Then there are those, seemingly rare occasions, when your guests are actually sleeping in one of your beds. The manager and I were touring his hotel one evening and as we went past a room, a woman started screaming. He used his emergency key to let us in. The room had a king-sized waterbed that for some reason had ruptured. The woman and her two-year-old daughter were asleep. The woman was very drunk, and trying to extract her daughter from the water and soggy linens but was actually making things worse for the two-year-old. The manager wrestled the hysterical mother to the floor, being mauled in the process, while I managed to get the baby out of the tangled mess in the bed before she drowned.

In one hotel near a naval training base, one of the major sources of business was the recruits on weekend leave. Of course, they did much of what you would expect, drinking, looking for dates, and so on. On my first visit to take supervision of this hotel, I found myself behind an attractive middle-aged lady checking in. While she was registering, someone asked if she would like to do something. It was a more vulgar version of, "Hey lady, want to have sex?" Now, there were only the three of us in the lobby; the woman, the desk clerk, and me. She turned to me and gave me a look that would have wilted a large pine tree. When it happened a second time, she clobbered me with her purse, which must have contained a small anvil, and stormed out. The desk clerk thought the whole thing was very funny as I picked myself up off the floor. It seems that the naval cadets had another pastime. They spent a lot of time teaching a myna bird some navy slang. The bird was in a large cage around the corner in a game room and he had a very broad vocabulary of profanity. Why couldn't the recruits just drink and sleep! I told the manager to ditch the bird. I don't know what happened to it. Even a zoo wouldn't take it with that mouth.

Occasionally your *guests* may not really be your guests. It sometimes happens that a bellman takes a newly registered guest to the assigned room to find someone else already occupying it. That can be the result of a screw up at the front desk, but more often, an unregistered guest occupies the room. He may have checked out, then decided to stay and had not informed the desk. Or he may have found or bought a key to the room.

One of the more bizarre cases evolved like this.

In one of my middle of the night tours of the hotel, I found myself in the sub-basement of the building. I caught a glimpse of a man going down a manhole cover in the floor that led to the utility feed tunnel. I followed him, down six metal steps to a tunnel, which was about five feet high and four feet wide. He went down this tunnel a short way and disappeared. I followed, peeking around a corner into a hollowed out room about six feet long and three feet wide. The man was living there. He was eating out of our dumpster and had confiscated some discarded linens to make a sleeping pallet. I went back to my office and called the police. They took him to a homeless shelter, and I installed a chain and padlock on the manhole cover.

CHAPTER XIII

Do I Have to do Everything Myself?

T he short answer to that question is, yes and no.

By now, I may have given you the impression that the manager is a one-man show and has to do everything himself. Well, I'm sorry about that, but some days it will seem like it's true. You will often say to yourself, "Damn, do I have to do everything?" Well, no you don't. However, don't lose site of the old saying, "Inspect what you expect."

In a full service hotel, you will have a few dozen to a few hundred employees, depending on the size, business volume, and complexity of the hotel. You cannot manage all those people personally. It is a struggle just to know their first names with the high turnover rate.

It has been my experience that you cannot personally manage more than twelve people. That is why you have department heads, which have unit managers, who in turn have section or shift supervisors.

No, you do not have to personally cook the food every day,

serve 3,000 dinners at a banquet, and clean all the rooms. What you do have to do personally is insure that it is all done, and done well consistently. So, how do you do that?

The first part of that answer goes back to knowing yourself. Know what you are good at and use it. Where you are not good, hire the best expertise you can find. You are not, and never will be, good at everything. You can learn something from everyone you meet. Accept it and use it.

I tried to replace a leaky flush valve in a toilet once. After multiple trips to the hardware store for tools and parts, and two floods in the bathroom, I finally called a plumber. He had the thing fixed in about fifteen minutes and told me that if I had called him before I made a mess of the job, I could have saved $60 of his bill. I no longer try to do plumbing.

You cannot, nor should you try to, inspect every steak delivered to your kitchen. But, you need to know enough about cuts and quality of meat to know when the person you are hiring to do that job knows what he is doing. You must also spot check his work to be sure he is doing the job, and not on a vendors payroll, as well as on yours.

As a management trainee, I was once assigned to act as purchasing agent while that person was out sick. The vendors approached me and asked if they could have the same deal with me as they had with Mr. S. I said sure. I immediately started getting short shipments of food product with little envelopes of money for me. When I reported this turn of events to the manager, Mr. S. was fired.

You cannot clean every room; buy all the room supplies and every replacement vacuum cleaner personally. But you need to approve the specifications for everything from cleaning supplies to the quality of toilet paper. You need to know what is "clean" as a guest defines it and spot check rooms with your Executive Housekeeper to assure that definition is being followed.

You cannot interview all applicants and hire every line employee. However, a new employee should be brought to your office for an introduction. That makes the new employee feel important and part of the family. It also lets you call him or her by name the next day, which goes a long way to reducing theft and turnover. (Employees are less likely to steal from a hotel where they feel they know the manager and the manager knows them.) They are less likely to show up drunk, or not at all. They are less likely to gut or strangle one of their co-workers, at least while on duty. You also hope they are less likely to hit you over the head with a table leg.

It goes without saying that you cannot cook and plate every dinner, and serve every guest personally. But, you need to know good food, when a plate of food looks desirable, and which side the fork goes on.

Well, you get the point about what you cannot do. So what can you do?

You must be visible and accessible. You will be dragged into things like I have related above when the situation is dangerous, or is beyond what you can reasonable expect your staff to handle.

You must hire, train, and supervise your department heads. They will report directly to you. Hire the best people you can find. Have a weekly staff meeting with them to keep them all informed and on the same page of the playbook. Train them to know everything that you know, particularly about managing people. The better they are, the easier your job will be. Always give your staff credit when things go well. Never take that credit for yourself. You will be the beneficiary in the end.

I once had a Regional Manager who had outstanding technical skills. His people skills were terrible. I worked with him to improve in that area, but it never fully took root. I finally had to replace him. Everyone you hire will come to the job with certain strengths and weaknesses. Exploit their skills and work to improve the weak areas. However, when the cost of the deficiencies outweighs the benefit of the strengths, it is time to part company.

Insist on cross training employees. It allows you to move people around to avoid boredom. It also allows flexibility in filling sudden gaps. Unless you like getting up at 11 p.m. to do the night audit, you had best be sure that every desk clerk can to that job, and the night manager and night security officer, too (if you have those).

As mentioned before, always establish a "Manager on Duty" program. This is where a department head is made the manager on duty for a week. This is rotated among your various department heads. It not only reduces your middle of the night calls, it gives your department managers a much broader understanding of what their peers deal with on a daily basis. Your food and beverage director will be exposed to front desk problems, engineering issues, and so on. He or she will be a better manager because of it, and more promotable, too.

Compliment in public; criticize in private. I cannot stress this rule too much. I was once Executive Assistant to a GM who did the opposite. (The same one I bailed out of jail.) He made a point of picking one person at every staff meeting to berate in front of the person's peers. Talk about wrecking morale at the highest level. Of course, that problem had the trickle down effect and our staff was completely demoralized. I learned more from this man about how not to manage people than could ever be related here.

I once worked for a woman who had the personality of a rabid rattlesnake. (I know that snakes don't usually get rabies, but I think this one did.) I saw her call the Executive Chef and General Manager to the podium at a banquet for 500 people. She berated them in very foul language and fired them both in front of the 500 people. Talk about instant morale problems. Some years later, the woman was in a lawsuit. Her lawyer offered $20,000 to me if I would be a character witness on her behalf. I declined, being hesitant to perjuring myself.

Another item to keep in mind is to control your anger. Never fire or discipline a person when you are mad. You will do and say things that will get you into trouble. It is best to suspend them and tell them to see you in the morning.

Get into the guts of your operation. Go down and spend fifteen minutes helping the dishwasher rack dishes. You will get to understand what he goes through for eight hours of every day and why that position has a high turnover rate. He will also feel like he is important to you and the breakage will drop off sharply. I should warn you, though, that you should do this only after telling the F&B Manager and the Executive Chef what you are going to do, and why. You don't want to undercut their positions. You will also find that they will follow your example. "Monkey see, monkey do." People will follow your lead, so lead well.

One day over lunch with a two star general, we got into the issue of managing people. He said that leading from the rear is like pushing a rope uphill. By the very definition of the word, it implies that you have to be in the front. He observed that one of the hardest parts of being a good leader was taking good care of your people. I said, "Are you kidding me? You send your people over the next hill to be shot, while telling another bunch to jump out of a perfectly good airplane at 5,000 feet." He responded that before he did that, he made sure his ground troops were properly trained and equipped, to lessen the chances of their being shot, and made sure the guys in the planes had good parachutes and knew how to use them.

If you learn that a suite has been completely trashed by the group that just checked out, get your Executive Housekeeper to go with you to the suite. Help the maid bag up the 141 beer bottles, and clean the carpet. That half hour will pay huge benefits not just with that maid, but with the entire housekeeping staff. Lead already.

Problem: Service is bogging down in the bar, but you are not doing enough volume to require a second bartender. Go down with your F&B Manager and help the bartender. You will find the problem. If it isn't a bad bartender, then it is probably the layout of the bar. Fix it.

I said that you must be accessible. That is true regarding both your guests and your employees. Most guest-related problems can and will be satisfactorily handled by your staff. (That is, if you have properly trained them and empowered them to fix the problems.) However, for those situations that they can't resolve, you need to be accessible to do so.

Employees are people. People have problems. Some of an employee's problems will be job related, some are personal (remember quiet desperation) that spill over to poor attitude and poor performance on the job, and then they become your problems. Be accessible. That does not mean that every employee should be able to come into your office and complain about his wife or about how his supervisor treats him. Employees must not be allowed to jump the chain of command; it will undercut your management team. One undesirable side effect of your having spent fifteen minutes with the dishwasher is that he may want to deal directly with you.

When an employee comes to you with a problem, refer them to their supervisor and tell the supervisor you did so. Telling the supervisor is a necessity. Anyone that has had kids knows the drill. They play Mommy and Daddy against each other. Adults are mostly kids who have outgrown their childhood clothes. They will try to play you and their supervisor against each other.

If the supervisor cannot or does not solve the problem, then you have the employee and the supervisor come to your office together to explore the situation and a resolution. A word of caution is in order here. Don't get sucked into fixing marital or family problems. You can never win in that kind of a situation. Refer them to a professional marriage councilor or some other appropriate professional. Even if you cannot solve their problem, you will get brownie points for listening and being understanding. Learn to be a better listener than talker. I believe that it was Mark Twain that, when asked why he talked so little said, "Better to keep your mouth shut and be thought a fool than to open it and remove all doubt". It has also been said that one learns more by listening than by talking. If you keep quiet, the other person will talk rather than just sit in silence with you staring at each other. You will learn things you didn't even know to ask about. This also works in contract negotiations.

Be visible to the employees on all shifts. I know that you would rather be sleeping (even if on an elevator) than going around the hotel at 3 a.m. However, doing that tour occasionally will pay big dividends with those employees on the graveyard shift. It also discourages those employees from sleeping on the job and going out on ledges. I once followed one of our night security guards on his rounds and found that he always rode the elevator. Thieves do not usually ride the elevator, preferring the stairwells as less trafficked areas. I insisted that he do likewise. Two nights later, he died in a stairwell from a heart attack. I didn't know he had a heart problem, honest.

Be visible to the guests. When I was a general manager, I tried to make time at least one day each week to be around the front desk or the front door to meet guests. They like doing business with a company where they can say they know the manager. They, like your employees, like to feel appreciated and important. It is best not to do that when things are in an uproar. There are enough problems hanging in the wings without you getting into the middle of it and making it worse.

Most managers do a poor job of being visible to guests. One way to meet some of the guests is to have a manager's cocktail party one evening each week. (I have seen many hotels where this is in place. Unfortunately, in too many cases the manager never shows up at the event.) This gives guests and the manager an opportunity to greet each other, the guests to make observations to the manager, and the manager to show his appreciation to them. If you listen with an open mind, you will even get some good ideas from your guests. If done well, the party improves guest utilization of the hotel restaurants, too. The party should feature your house wine (private label if you have one) and hors d'oeuvres from one of your restaurants.

One evening when we were having horrid service problems in our fine dining restaurant, my boss's wife jumped in to take a station and help serve. Things got even worse. After the dining room closed, I called a meeting of the staff to determine what caused the service problems. The service staff said they couldn't get food out of the kitchen. My boss's wife said she didn't think that was the problem, since she had not had trouble getting her orders filled. One waiter said, "Of course not, they filled you orders and ours got backed up even more." Don't make things worse by trying to help.

Stand at the restaurant door occasionally and introduce yourself to guests. Wish them a happy evening and tell them that if they have any suggestions for your restaurant, to pass them along to you or your staff.

Have your chef go through the dining room, preferably in a clean uniform, and visit each table. He should ask if they have any suggestions. Some lady may say that perhaps a little less garlic in the garlic mashed potatoes. The chef writes that down. She will come back soon to see if there is less garlic in the potatoes. Of course, there probably won't be, (if you have standardized receipts) but she will be sure there is, just because the chef cared enough to ask.

If you want to build repeat business in the dining room, try this; have your chef or restaurant manager go through the dining room with a tray of small servings of some dish that you are going to add to the menu. Tell the guests that you are considering adding this dish to the menu and would like their opinion. They will come back often, bringing their friends, proudly telling them that they suggested that item. Manage your guests.

Solve problems before they become problems. Stand in the dining room and watch. If you see a table of four where the service is sluggish, send them a bottle of the wine they are having, or an assortment of appetizers, complimentary. They will be your customers forever, you have avoided a guest complaint, and it only cost you $8 instead of having to write off dinner for four, or worse, losing repeat business. The most expensive loss to you from a guest problem is from the one that is never reported.

Some guests will complain to you in person, some by mail. In either case, you need to show some compassion. I remember a situation that happened a few months after Amtrak took over the passenger train system. A passenger wrote a letter of complaint to Amtrak about cockroaches in his compartment. In a few days, he got a very nice letter from one of their executives telling how hard they were working to correct such conditions and how much they appreciated his informing them of the problem. He noticed a paper clip with a hand written note on the back of the letter. The note was from the executive to his secretary. It said, "Send this stupid SOB the standard cockroach letter." Never use form letters to answer a complaint. The guest will spot it and you have just made things worse by telling him that he isn't important enough for you to write a personal response. A brief hand written note is always more impressive than a typed formal letter.

Be accessible and be visible. These employees and guests will make you or break you.

Again, always make your employees and your boss look good. You will be the beneficiary for it.

CHAPTER XIV

WHAT ABOUT BIG PROBLEMS?

So, you are getting bored with these little petty problems of staffing guides and suicides, are you? Do you think you are ready to tackle some bigger stuff?

I mentioned earlier that one of the biggest terrors of any hotel manager who still has his or her sanity by now is a hotel fire. It is one of the most feared events in a hotel.

I witnessed a hotel fire early in my career. Fortunately for me, it was a hotel that I had nothing to do with. I was just one in the crowd, standing on a street corner at 10 p.m. watching.

This was a major fire in a major hotel. I watched the frantic efforts of the heroic firemen. I watched the smoke and flames billowing out of the roof and windows. I watched people jump to their deaths as their clothing left flaming paths in the smoky air. I watched as panicked people climbed out on ledges, ten stories above the street. I watched as some of them fell. I watched, as over 200 people died horrible deaths. I stood there all night and watched as firemen carried out the bodies of charred adults and children. I stood there all night and cried. I left the next morning with a full understanding of what a hotel fire is like. I have never gotten over the horror of a hotel fire.

My first scare about a hotel fire happened in a 650-room hotel where I was the Resident Manager. We had just installed a new fire alarm system. The contractor took me to the control panel, showed me how it worked, how to shut it off, and how to re-set it. Two nights later, it sounded at 3:30 a.m. That is as close to panic as I have ever been or ever want to be.

I had some 450 people, plus my family, sleeping in that hotel. By the time I had grabbed some clothing, and run down the stairs to the lobby, people were streaming out into the street in various states of nightwear, in towels, or with sheets wrapped around them. Fire trucks were arriving by all entrances, hoses were being unrolled and hooked to pumper trucks, ladder trucks were unhooking their ladders, and ambulances were screaming down the street. There was panic everywhere. I ran to the basement to turn off the alarm, which was causing even more panic. The damned thing wouldn't shut off. I ran to the engineer's office, kicked in the door, grabbed some wire cutters, and cut the wires. (I learned later that one of the contractor's employees had changed the code and didn't tell me.) False alarm! I had many angry guests, but at least I didn't have any injured or dead ones. I had nightmares for nights afterward. In later years, I lived in a large hotel near the central fire station. Every time a truck went out at night I woke with the sweats and could not go back to sleep, even after the trucks passed my hotel.

I dealt with several hotel fires in kitchens, laundries, guest rooms, and storerooms. Fortunately, none of them were major.

Fires are not the only big problems. I got a call early one evening that the transformer room was flooding. Our transformer room was the central feed point for all the electrical service for the hotel, which was nineteen stories high and covered the better part of a square city block. The room was two levels below ground and had four transformers the size of Jeep Wranglers, with very high voltage. These transformers sat on concrete pads about three feet off the floor. A four-inch water main had ruptured near that room and water was pouring in. Per our emergency plan, the fire department, the water department, and the electric company had been called and were arriving. We all went to the sub-basement to find over two feet of water in the room. None of the personnel of the three groups would wade into the water to kill the main switches on the far wall. To make matters worse, the fire chief was insisting that the hotel be evacuated. Not only would toilets not flush, and there was no fire fighting system functional, but if the transformers exploded, we could lose much of the building and many of the people in it.

I dispatched my trusty Executive Assistant to round up all the staff she could find, assign sections to them, and start getting guests out of the building (via the stairs of course). Still no one would go into the water, which was still inching up toward those four bombs. I stripped off my shoes, socks, and pants, and waded through the water to kill the main feed switches. Was that heroic or stupid? Probably neither and probably some of both, but I did what I felt I must in a crisis.

Short of fire, broken water lines are the biggest source of property damage. In one such instance, we blew a water main in the ceiling of a new luxury restaurant that was due to open the next day. The restaurant had $450,000 worth of art, furniture, flocked wallpaper, gold leaf, and carpets. When I arrived on the scene, there was nearly a foot of water in the sunken floor. We got the main turned off and called the fire department for a pumper truck to start sucking water out. (Always get to know the mayor, police chief, and fire chief in your city.) By working around the clock, we got open on time.

At one point in my career, I was the supervising general manager of three hotels. That meant I managed one, and supervised the general managers of the other two. I was in one of these hotels one night when there was a teeth jarring explosion.

Grabbing my pants, I ran down to the lobby where I met the GM and an assortment of other employees and guests, all in a dither.

This was an older hotel, and had not been well maintained by prior owners. Three rooms on the fourth floor had dropped to the floor below. One man was still sitting on his toilet, now in room 306 instead of 406. Surprisingly, there were no deaths, only a few broken bones, cuts, and bruises. (Memo to myself: Call the lawyer first thing in the morning.)

How about this to make your day? One resort that we managed sat in a northern city and at the edge of the mountains. The drive under the marquee was raised above a wing of facing rooms. At 2 a.m., a guest pulled up to the main entrance in his big Caddy. The driver went into the lobby, leaving the car running. For some reason, the accelerator linkage snapped and the big V8 engine revved to the maximum, catapulting the car through the air at the down side of the grade and into the plate glass sliding door of a room on the second floor. While that stopped the flying car on top of a bed and killed the engine, it also blew the fuel tank, which in turn blew out several nearby windows and several people out of their beds. The man in the room was saved because he had just gone into his bathroom and therefore escaped being between his mattress and the front third of a Cadillac. (Was it my guardian angel or his that I saw limping down the road?) Memo to myself: Call our lawyer in the morning.

CHAPTER XV

WHO NEEDS TRAINING TO CLEAN A TOILET?

O ne would think that anyone could clean a toilet. Not true, at least not to the standard that you must have in a hotel. Yes, any dope can swirl a brush around in the toilet bowl, but that isn't cleaning it. You must have all surfaces cleaned, and sanitized, including the ones that can only be seen by sitting in the tub, and the hinges on lids. So the maids, those than inspect rooms, your Executive Housekeeper, and you need training. I have had some outstanding executives as Executive House-keepers, but I have never seen one sitting in a bathtub or lying on the floor looking under a bed until I trained them to do so.

They also seldom look under chair and sofa cushions, but the guests do. I had one manager who would sometimes leave a $5 bill under a cushion and then went with the housekeeper to look under it after the room had been serviced. If the money was still there, the maid was called back to the room. If the $5 was missing, but had not been turned in, the maid was cautioned. If the maid found it and turned it in, she got a $10 reward.

You also have to sanitize the bathroom floor. I once found a maid mopping the bathroom floor by using the water in the toilet bowl. Oh, yuck!

Cleaning the room includes under the bed, behind the desk, the picture frames, and the windowsill, as well as checking all drawers for items left behind. If you want to lose a guest, leave a hair in the bathtub, or a dirty sock or pair of underwear under the bed. The A/C filter is the most missed item in a cleaning schedule. Dirty air filters not only make for dirty rooms, they run your utility bill out the roof. However, a maintenance man or houseman usually does this on a monthly basis. You also need to rotate the mattresses on a quarterly basis to extend their life.

There is a right and wrong way to rack dishes. Kitchens must be sanitized, not just mopped. Grills, broilers, and ovens must be cleaned. Restaurant and ballroom carpets must be shampooed. The filters on your laundry dryers must be cleaned daily. Lint in these is like gunpowder and one of the most common causes of fire. Employees and supervisors must all be trained to meet your standards.

Serving food is not just delivering it to the table and asking who gets the fried chicken. There is a right and wrong way to set the table, to serve the food, and to pick up the soiled dishes. There is a right and wrong way to open and serve a bottle of wine.

One of my pet peeves is having a waiter ask who gets a particular plate of food. It tells the guests and me at the table, that we are not important enough for the server to care who ordered what. I learned a lesson from a good waiter about how to keep orders straight for any number of people. I picked up one of his tickets in the kitchen one evening and the second item on the ticket was "bald fish." I asked him, "What the devil is a bald fish"? (Another of his orders said "Red pork chop.") He said the bald man ordered the fish. He wrote the orders counterclockwise from the bald man and at the other table from the lady in the red dress. That way, he knew where every plate went, even though he served the ladies first.

I loved hiring retired Pullman waiters from trains. Now those guys knew service. I once hired one who never wrote anything down while at the table. People used to come in six to ten at a table and try to confuse him, by changing their orders, and so on. I thought he had a phenomenal memory until I caught his trick. After taking orders, he went into the kitchen and wrote up the order for the cooks. He wore a small tape recorder.

All your employees and all their supervisors must be trained. You can't expect them to do it right unless you teach them what right is, as you define it. Having trained them, you now have to motivate them to do it. I mentioned early on that everyone has "hot buttons." Recognize them and use them. Make their hot buttons match your needs. A simple example is that a waitress makes most of her money by getting tips. Show her that doing it your way will greatly increase her tips. Then, she is far more likely to do it your way, rather than doing it just because you *said* to do it that way.

In between writing staffing guides and employee manuals, specifying vacuum cleaners, and entertaining an NFL quarterback for lunch, you need to write training manuals. Get your department heads and unit managers to help. They are going to be more inclined to use them if they had a hand in writing them, rather than you just passing them down the chain of command. Also, keep in mind that you are not, and cannot be, an expert on everything. Their input is essential. Train your people, but don't get such a big head that you can't also learn from them. Everyone you deal with can teach you something. Ask your people for their ideas, even the line employees. Who knows more about racking dishes than the dishwasher? You will both learn a lot, and you will get bonus points for flattering them enough to ask.

To compound your training problems, keep in mind that you will have to re-train sixty to seventy percent of your staff every year due to high turnover. While working to reduce turnover, you should identify where the bulk of that is occurring. You will probably find that a handful of jobs create the bulk of your turnover problems. Some of the most common areas of high turnover are in dishwashers, pot washers, maids, kitchen and night cleaners, and worst of all, in cooks. See what you can do to make those jobs more desirable. Some of those things may be better tools, cushioned floor mats for cooks, more frequent breaks, and job rotation. Racking dishes, once mastered gets quite boring after a few days. Rotate that guy with one in another job monthly and of course cross train them. Giving him a chance for promotion to salad prep will also help. Promote from within as much as possible, but not too much. (Discouraging the cooks from gutting each other will also help.)

When I started my own management company, I decided that I would always try to promote from within. What I found in a couple of years was that I was starting to breed idiots. It was like incest. No one ever had a good or new idea. They only knew what they knew and we needed new blood with new ideas. The other thing to avoid is taking the easy way out. The best waitress does not necessarily make the best dining room manager.

CHAPTER XVI

WHY NOT GO OFFSHORE?

I t seemed to be a natural extension of our management contract services to go to the Caribbean Islands and perhaps to
South or Central America. They certainly needed some better
management in most of their hotels.

My first move in this direction was to take a consulting job on
the north shore of the Dominican Republic. A small international
chain wanted to buy a site near Puerto Plata to develop an all-
inclusive resort. The bank didn't agree that it was a good location.
The bank hired me to look at the site, and if good, to draft an
agreement between the chain and the bank.

I took my in-house lawyer and a member of the chain, and flew
into Santo Domingo. We chartered a plane to Puerto Plata. The
plane was to make another run and come back for us between 5
p.m. and 6 p.m. When it still had not arrived at 8 p.m., we called
the charter service to learn that it had crashed in the mountains
that run across the island. We rented a car to drive back to the
south side of the island.

The Dominican Republic at that time did not have the prolif-
eration of gas stations, and rest stops so common in the US. By
9 p.m., we were starving, and we stopped at a roadside stand for

some fried plantains and beer. The only beer they had were quart sized. After drinking that, we all needed a rest stop, but there were none. I pulled over to the shoulder of the road, high in the mountains. The lawyer stepped out of the car and promptly disappeared with a scream. We ran around the car to find the right wheels were inches from a cliff. The lawyer had stepped out into thin air and was hanging about three feet down, from a scrubby tree. We finally got him to the top of the cliff, but found he no longer needed a restroom.

I went later to another site in the same area for another client. Not trusting to the charter planes, and feeling that I knew the road, I rented a car. The drive north was uneventful since it was daytime. However, on the way back south that night, I took a wrong turn and wound up at a voodoo ceremony in Haiti.

Undeterred by these events, I next ventured to Venezuela. My first effort here was to look into the proposed development of a hotel by the government. This was my first real exposure to dealing with the members of a foreign culture. I found they work from 10 a.m. to 2 p.m. and then took siesta until about 8 p.m. Then they have dinner and talk until 2 a.m.

The first morning, I ordered breakfast and coffee. The waiter asked in Spanish, which I don't speak, if I wanted milk or sugar. I declined and he retreated a few steps to wait. My first sip of their black coffee created the bald spot on my head. Without a word, the waiter came over to the table and quietly added hot milk.

At lunch with the government official at his country club one day, I noticed that every tee and hole had a uniformed man with a shotgun. I asked my host if they took a dim view of bad golfers. He smiled and said the men didn't shoot bad golfers; they were there to keep the riffraff from coming from the shanties on the mountainsides down to the golf course. The proposed hotel never was built, because shortly after my third visit, the government official was shot.

I then tried a private developer planning a resort on the east coast of Venezuela. That deal never materialized because the developer was kidnapped. I decided that Venezuela was probably not a healthy place to do business and took management of a resort in Martinique.

The resort was on the French side of the island. While it may upset some people, I can say with some validity that doing business with the French is as much frustration as one ever wants to be immersed in.

The resort was in serious financial trouble when we took it. At the bank, we were always overdrawn by $800,000 or more. If our over drafts got to $1,000,000 they called and asked us to please make a deposit. Try that in the good old USA.

I found that we couldn't cut the staff, though the property was grossly overstaffed. We needed four people in the accounting office, but had thirty on the payroll, and twelve desks in the office. An employee hired without an employment agreement was deemed hired for life.

To make it even worse, one never knew from day to day who would show for work. It was law, not union contract that an employee who wanted to miss work could take a note to the chief of police saying that he was on strike until further notice. When he tired of fishing, sleeping, drinking, or whatever, he collected the note and came to the hotel to report to work. While he was "on strike," he got half-pay. Therefore, in every department, every day, no matter who was scheduled to work, you had to manage with whoever showed up.

Some days when you needed eight waiters, you had two, and some days fifteen. It was a royal mess.

I got a call one morning from the head of the union at the local power plant. He informed me that they were going on strike and he would like me to tell our union to walk out in support of the strike. I declined. He told me that if I didn't cooperate, our power would not be turned back on when they went back to work. I responded that it would be a big favor to us if they didn't turn it on, since we had the only large generator on the island, and I could make power cheaper than buying theirs.

After a few months, I canceled our contract in Martinique. It was just too frustrating and we could not manage within their legal and cultural framework.

I limited our further off shore ventures to the US Virgin Islands and Puerto Rico. We did consulting on several hotels in Puerto Rico, but did not take full management control of any.

I found that doing business with the power base in Puerto Rico a true pleasure. They were generous to a fault and genteel. They collected you from the airport in a stretch limo, took you to your hotel suite, complete with fruit basket and champagne, sometimes even with a personal maid.

When collected and taken to their office, you were greeted with coffee and chocolates.

They were always polite and cooperative, even to working on a schedule that you were comfortable with. Siestas be damned.

However, if you find yourself working with them, do not be deceived. They are tough business people. They will negotiate you down to splitting coins, but they do it with a smile, politeness, and hot chocolate.

CHAPTER XVII

WHERE THE HELL AM I?

The management company started, as I said, as a subsidiary of a company that had foreclosed on six motels, hotels, and resorts. The parent company wanted to sell them, and over the years, we did. Obviously, that was good for the company, bad for my job security. So we formed a wholly owned subsidiary to seek management contracts from other sources. Over a four-year period, we shrank the owned properties to one, but added twenty-five management contracts. Over the next two years, we floated between twenty-five and thirty properties in the managed portfolio. I then bought the management company and took it private.

This turn of events brought a completely new learning curve beyond personally managing a small number of properties. I found that I now had to get results by working through a couple of regional managers and a bunch of General Managers. It was a lot harder than having a direct hands-on capability. My job now consisted of being on the road four or five days of every week. I was meeting with owners, seeking new contracts, looking at potential properties, and inspecting our managed properties.

After a few months of staying in twenty to thirty hotel rooms in that many cities every month, I learned a lot.

The first thing was that when I woke at about 4 a.m., in a strange room, in a strange city, I often didn't know where I was for a while. I developed the habit of leaving a note on the bedside table as to where I was. Thus, when I woke, I could read the note and find that I was in XYZ hotel, in a given city, and what day of the week it was. Now one may conclude from this that I was a bit senile. That wasn't the problem. It was just that all hotel rooms looked pretty much the same.

The typical room had a closet on one side of the entrance, with a bath across from it. The room bay would be twelve feet by twenty-four feet, give or take a couple of feet. The bed or beds and end tables were on one wall, usually the same side as the bath, with a couple of cheap pictures screwed to the wall over the headboards. On the other wall were a chest with a TV on it and a desk that was too small to be useable and a desk chair. The room was usually decorated in earth tones. The end result was that when waking at 4 a.m. after five or six hours sleep, you could be anywhere. By leaving a note to myself, I avoided the embarrassment of calling the front desk and asking, "Where the hell am I, and what day is it?"

That question usually got the response of, "Are you all right?" By the time the 7 a.m. employees arrived, they all knew that the guest in my room was daft, drunk, badly hung over, or perhaps considering suicide.

When we built our first owned hotel, I had a list of things that I wanted to do differently. While the general size and shape of the room bay was largely dictated by construction costs, the interior wasn't. I put more light in the bathrooms with a built in night light. The bath also had a make-up mirror and a vanity stool. If you are a woman who travels or if you have traveled with a woman, you know how important these things are.

I designed a corner headboard and angled the bed into a corner behind the bath. The triangular headboard had two inlaid pieces of cork to set drinks on. One of the big maintenance problems in hotels is from guests setting sweating glasses on the end tables, which wrecks the finish. That freed up a lot of floor space, which allowed a workable-sized desk, a decent desk chair, and a recliner. I ditched the common practice of earth tones in carpets, drapes, bedspreads, and wall coverings. We went with mauve, green, and blue. Now we had 225 rooms that a guest didn't have to leave a note in to be sure where he was.

We also used fitted bedspreads. I had learned long ago that a coverlet and bed skirt was a problem. More often than not, the bed skirt was askew and was frequently grabbed by the vacuum cleaner, which promptly chewed on it.

Of course, I had also learned that a given hotel had to define its market(s) to be successful. Now I learned to think outside the box.

One property had a wing of very tiny guest rooms. These were added during WWII, as had been done in many hotels of that era. The rooms were virtually unsalable in the current market. However, several large companies in the city needed rooms to house their staff in town for training. The companies needed rooms that could handle two trainees to keep costs down. However, the standard double room had one bath and one small desk. We removed every other wall in this wing of small rooms. That created a large room with two baths, two beds, and two good-sized desks. That wing of rooms soon ran the highest occupancy in the hotel. At the end of the hall on each floor, we combined several rooms to make training rooms.

In another hotel, we built a tiered theater. The seating was all swivel armchairs. (One mega-company has the stated belief that the mind can absorb only as much as the butt can endure.) The desks had an under shelf for purses, lap top cases, and other paraphernalia. In the back of the room, we installed a small room that opened on both sides. From the hall we could set up coffee breaks without disturbing the meeting or tying up another meeting room for the break. When the coffee break was ready, we turned on a small green light. Thus, the person at the podium knew when to call a break. The coffee room had three sets of wood-slatted doors that went into the ceiling, opening the entire area to the theater side.

In another convention hotel, we had a shortage of suites of various sizes. The existing suites were at the ends of hallways with one or two bedrooms. We installed a wall/door system on tracks in the hall. We could move these down the hall, latch them into place, and create suites of up to six bedrooms.

One thing you learn very quickly in the hotel business is that your hotel restaurant(s) cannot flourish by serving hotel guests alone. You must find a way to tap the local market, too. That isn't easy when every town of 30,000 residents or more has a long list of restaurants. They offer everything from fast food to upper end dining. To make matters worse for you, most hotel restaurants are not known for fine food, or even for good value. Of course, as in any generalization, there are exceptions, but historically hotel restaurants have generally done a poor job of making a mark in the local market.

In one hotel, we had a four star, four-diamond restaurant. After some months, it began to flag in its penetration of the local market. We changed the menu, that didn't work. We changed the concept of the restaurant. That didn't help much either.

In all my moving around, I had learned that every town and city has its own micro-culture. Always, a handful of men and women are "movers and shakers." These people may be bankers, lawyers, doctors, or major business executives, but not always. Sometimes they have considerable sway in the community without being high profile. One may be the head of the PTA.

Another may be the music director of a church or a nun. They are not necessarily rich or political figures. We needed to tap these people for our struggling restaurant.

We started a "chef's table." Every Sunday evening, we set a table for five in the spotlessly clean kitchen. It had starched white table linens with a waiter in a tuxedo. This was a full seven-course meal down to the intermezzo. We invited four of the local leaders to dinner with our Executive Chef. During dinner, the chef, in a white starched uniform and tall chef's hat, explained the menu and the preparation methods. Each guest went away with a bottle of our private label wine. After three or four weeks, we had people calling to see how they could get an invitation to the chef's table. Being at the chef's table became a status symbol in the community. In a month, our local business had tripled.

A side story here about this restaurant. It only seated sixty-eight people, so we could do a lot of table side service like a true Caesar Salad and Bananas Foster. One of the things we did was to bring a cart to each table with an assortment of uncooked entrees for the patrons to pick from. These included fine steaks, chops, live lobsters, and other options. One evening a two-pound lobster escaped, undetected, from the cart and went under a table. It began to play with a lady's toes through her open-toed shoes. Thinking it to be an untimely itch, or that perhaps her husband was being a bit randy, she ignored it. However, when the lobster started climbing her leg she looked under the table. This brought a crystal-shattering scream and the lady jumped up, dumping the table china, wine glasses, water glasses, and all into the other woman's lap. This caused that woman to scream too. The whole restaurant became mass pandemonium. The other patrons, not being sure what the problem was, began jumping on tables and chairs, and running for doors. In the middle of this, we had two waiters crawling around on the floor trying to recapture the lobster without being trampled by the guests. The event made the front page of the local paper the next morning. It has been said that any press is good press, I'm not sure of that though.

Another thing I learned in all this traveling around had to do with inspecting the hotels we operated. Of course, I always let the GM of a hotel know that I was coming. He would assign a room for my overnight use. I never stayed in it. I knew that the room he had assigned was in the best shape of any in the hotel. The Executive Housekeeper had done a white glove inspection on it, as had the GM. I always requested a different room. When the General Managers figured that out they always prepared a back up. So, I got more specific. I asked the desk clerk for a room by the elevator, on a higher floor, or near the ice machine. If I had been assigned a king room, I asked for a double. If I was assigned a suite, I asked for a king.

In one hotel, I found upon my first day that there were a dozen very large cats roaming the kitchen. Now this didn't meet any health department code that I had ever encountered, so I told the Executive Chef to ditch the cats. He said that was going to be a big mistake, but he did it. Within a week, we had rats everywhere, including occasionally romping through the dining room. Guests tend to frown on dining with rats. It took the exterminating company weeks to fix what the cats had kept under control.

Our corporate staff never used the pools, exercise rooms, or golf courses. It gave the employees at the hotel, and the hotel owner the idea that we were vacationing instead of working. We also never accepted VIP gifts like fruit baskets. If one was put in my room and was very perishable, I told the desk clerk to send it to one of their regular guests with the compliments of the GM. Of course, the GMs were then told not to do that again.

We also had to be constantly on guard for employees who wanted to give you favors to get a raise, or a promotion, or just a good employee review rating. It was not uncommon for a female department head to try to play footsy under the conference table, or a chef who wanted to make a special meal for you. Then there was always the bartender who poured a double-sized drink. I have even had night turn-down maids offer "extra services" while turning down the bed. I have had bellmen offer to introduce me to a "special female friend of his" and once a prospective client sent his daughter to my room for siesta time.

Another hazard is that organized crime is always lurking near the fringes of the business. It has long been know of their involvement in gambling areas like Las Vegas, Reno, and Atlantic City. But they also hover around big hotels. I was once offered lots of cash to set up a money laundering scheme. In another case, I bailed out a high union official who had been caught in a prostitution sting. I got a phone number to call if I ever needed a favor. I used it several years later, and was told that the slate was now clean.

In a case that made the local newspaper and got several union and mafia figures tossed into jail, the company I worked for moved me to an obscure town and gave me a set of false IDs should I need them.

While I had considerable exposure by now to a multitude of owners, this exposure now broadened significantly. Some of them were really bizarre.

One owner, when visiting one of her hotels while I was there, asked me to retrieve a full set of new furniture from the warehouse. We were adding a twenty-eight-room addition with furnishings bought by the prior manager. The owner hated it and told me to pile all twenty-eight rooms of furniture in the parking lot and burn them. And I thought some guests were irrational. Of course, I didn't burn it.

Another owner was so explosive and argumentative that he kept our home office staff in a state of terror. At one owners' meeting in his hotel with our regional manager and marketing director, the owner was so worked up that he had an aneurism.

Our regional manager went out to the secretary and told her to call an ambulance. I told the regional manager later that the next time that happened to just close the meeting room door and go to the airport.

On one trip to Texas, our Director of Marketing witnessed a migration of tarantulas. She was very taken aback. Some days later, I went into my office to find it over run with crickets. After many pointed inquiries, I learned that the GM in Texas had sent a large hairy tarantula to our Director of Marketing. (I told you managers sometimes are a bit fried and their sense of humor tilts to the bizarre.) She and her graphic artist had installed it in a cage and named it after the owner just mentioned. The crickets-tarantula food-had chewed their way out of the cardboard container that housed them and were all over the offices. Very few of the home office staff had any desire to feed or water the tarantula. That became a problem on holiday weekends when no one was in the office. We finally gave the beast to my daughter's Montessori School. They renamed it Charlotte, from the book Charlotte's Web.

CHAPTER XVIII

So, What Was it Like in the "Good Old Days?"

To some who read this, the "good old days" will be remembered as the eighties or early nineties.

To some of us who are in walkers or using a cane, or close to it, those days are in the fifties or sixties or before. After all, the good old days are any days in the past that one recalls as being simpler and life was easier without today's problems.

Was life simpler and easier in hotels in the older, good old days? The short and easy answer is an unequivocally no. I remember agonizing for weeks over whether to raise room rates by twenty-five cents.

Now rates are changed by $10 or $70 on a daily or hourly basis with the stroke of a computer key. Pay rates were debated for long periods of time and union contracts negotiated over a two-cent versus a five-cent raise.

So, what were hotels like in the 1960s and before? Believe it or not, they were much tougher to manage. First, labor was relatively cheap, so hotels had a lot more employees than they do today. A 600-room hotel today may have 300 employees more or less, depending on complexity and business volume. Back then, the same hotel would have sported 400 or 500 employees.

I remember one upscale hotel in Chicago (similar to the Waldorf in NYC) that boasted sixty-four maintenance people. If that hotel existed, today it would have a maintenance staff of less than twenty. What did all those people do? Well, they manned the TV repair shop, the upholstery shop, the carpentry shop, an equipment repair shop, and a paint shop. Today, the smaller staff makes only minor repairs to equipment, does touch up painting, and so on. Large projects are contracted out. Televisions are sent to a TV repair shop or replaced. I don't know of any hotel today that does its own upholstery work.

Large city hotels built in the 1920s and before were often equipped to provide steam to much of the downtown area. They carried a fireman and engineer on every shift, much like a steam locomotive did. High-pressure boilers had to be monitored constantly.

When air conditioning was added to those hotels, central steam absorption compressors were added. Those units were huge; in the winter they were broken down, the tubes cleaned, and maintained. (Even though it has been explained to me repeatedly, I still don't know how cold air is made out of steam.)

The older central systems had a two-pipe system. That meant that you either ran hot water or cold water through the pipes. It took as much as eight to ten hours to change the system from heat to cool or from cool to heat. Spring and fall in much of the country finds cool nights needing heat and hot days needing A/C. To make matters worse, the rooms on the south side of the building may need A/C and not rooms on the north side. These conditions created many guest complaints. City and state codes also came to prohibit the ability to open windows in guest rooms, partly brought about by suicides and children falling out. Later, central systems were installed with a four-pipe system and individual air-handling units above the entrance ceiling of each guest room. That allowed a guest to choose his room temperature, no matter what the guy across the hall wants. Due to the cost of such a central system, most newer hotels have through the wall units.

The housekeeping departments used to make their own table linens, bedspreads, and drapes. Some even made their own uniforms. Today they buy them.

Kitchen staffs no longer bake their own bread and cakes. They don't make their own ice cream or butcher sides of beef either.

What was the worst job in the hotel of yesteryear? You may guess that it was pot washer, night cleaner, or maid. Not so. By far the worst job in old hotels was working in the laundry. As a management trainee, I spent thirty days in a large hotel laundry, way back when. It is as close to Hell as any mortal would want to get, and like the kitchens of the time, about as hot. Moreover, the laundry staff didn't get "cook's beer" every two hours.

The laundry had cranes that picked up baskets holding 300 or 400 pounds of dry linen, now weighing multiples of that, from the washers and placed them in huge extractors. From there, the crane delivered and dumped them into troughs in front of dryers. There each piece was taken by hand and loaded into the dryers. This linen was still hot and soaked with bleach. All the workers on this line had red and blistered hands and forearms. The hot dried linens were then removed piece by piece, and sorted by table linen, bed linen, and terry cloth. The table linen and bed linen went to a large ironer called a mangle. It was aptly named, since it had a huge appetite for the workers' fingers. There two women fed linen into the machine. Four women on the finish end caught the red-hot linen as it came out and folded it.

Uniforms were washed and dried in smaller machines, and then delivered to the ironers. These were usually elderly women, who stood on their feet all day, ironing the uniforms. Most of them had varicose veins and bad backs. A separate section in the laundry dry-cleaned drapes and those uniforms that required it.

The hotel laundry of today has no-iron bed and table linens and no mangle. Uniforms are sent out or even rented from a uniform supplier. Washer/extractors and dryers are larger versions of what you would have at home.

However, there are tradeoffs. Blankets and bedspreads aren't washed as often. Some hotels even give guests the option of not having the bed linen changed daily.

Hotel accounting offices have also changed. I managed one hotel where we had two clerks who did nothing except sort and band cash, and sort and roll coins. With the common use of credit cards, now many hotels have to go to a bank, or use a Brinks service to keep the right denominations of bills and coin on hand.

Even the night cleaning staff has shrunk. Now with a modern buffing machine, one man can clean and buff a hard surface floor where it took six before. Parking lots are cleaned by one man on a vacuum machine verses several with push brooms.

One person on a computer mans the reservation offices instead of several working on phones, and the front desk may have two clerks instead of a small army. Room inventory is controlled on a computer, in the "good old days" it was done by a stock card. Each card was about two inches by four inches, had a room number, and was sorted by type of room. When a room was rented, the card went from an available rack to a room rack with each slot having a room number on it.

Individual folios, or room accounts were made up by hand and charges posted by hand. The folio had three carbon slips on the front, with one going into the room rack and the other two going to the telephone department where they were placed in a rack by room number and alphabetically. I don't know of a single hotel today that staffs a telephone switchboard (called a PBX for Private Branch Exchange).

Kitchen staffs are also smaller. Many hotels buy salad greens already cleaned, chopped and diced. Convection ovens have reduced cooking times and better machines have reduced the need for as many dishwashers and pot washers.

I have managed two hotels that had separate kitchens for just preparing food for the Jewish clientele. These Kosher kitchens also had their own set of pots, pans, china, flatware, and so on.

The food service staff and the rooms housekeeping staff remain largely the same. Food still has to be moved from the kitchen to the table. Tables still have to be cleared for the next patrons. It still takes a given amount of time to clean a guest room.

The only good news about the hotels of yesteryear was that people needed jobs, since the government "welfare" programs were not as generous, and people had a much better work ethic. I have actually had employees tell me that they couldn't work for me anymore, since they could make more by staying home.

The one department that is probably larger than before is security. So, modern manager, take heart. Things could be worse.

CHAPTER XIX

So Now What?

O kay, now you have worked your way up through the hotel ranks and it is time to take stock of your situation.

You have turned several hopeless hotels into moneymakers. You have provided countless people with a fine dinner and a successful business meeting or convention. You have given thousands of people a place of refuge from their worries and travels, some of them may even have used your comfortable beds to sleep in.

You have helped thousands more become successful in their jobs and careers. You have even staffed some of your competitors' hotels with them before you figured out how to retain them. You have paid for a handful of high-potential employees to go to rehabilitation clinics and one or two to shrinks.

In the process of doing all this, you have lost that naive attitude you came into the business with. The high morals you started out with have been tamped firmly under some carpet along the way. You have had your rosy opinion of people trampled into the dust. You no longer believe that bad things don't happen to good people. You have probably wrecked more than one marriage, some of them your own, and had untold numbers of people thrown in jails around the country. You have bailed some out and left others to rot. You have fought with some, loved others, and been disappointed by many.

You have missed many emotional highs, but avoided even more emotional lows, while you cowered in your emotional castle.

You have gained and lost enough weight in your life to make two more people. (I once opened a gourmet dining room in a hotel. To get the menu and recipes right, I ate a seven-course meal twice each day for thirty days and then entertained guests in the room for twenty-six of the next thirty days. I gained eighty pounds and lost it over the next few months.)

At one point, you got a fine set of stomach ulcers and learned the true meaning of "It is better to give than to receive."

The comets streaking through your life have been moments of delight and moments of despair and even awe.

So, in taking further stock of your life, you discover that you have bags under your eyes, some of your hair is falling out, and the rest of it is turning gray. You don't get enough exercise, you smoke too much, and if you had time, you would probably eat and drink too much.

The good news is that you haven't been killed or maimed yet, and you don't recall having killed anyone else, in spite of the urge to do so from time to time. Though you have had a couple of people die in your arms.

The bad news is that you can't really count on your guardian angel. He or she (do guardian angels have a sex?) is probably a total wreck by now and in far worse shape than you are.

Not too bad, with all things considered. So you take a deep breath and think that finally you can have that nice lunch and a scotch and water by the pool. Your new job as Divisional Manager of a large management company should provide you with some time for that.

Think again. You now have fifty hotel owners calling you and asking for meetings with you. This one says his wife's bridge club had poor service and he wants you to look into it personally. The next one says he is leaving his company and wants to introduce you to his replacement.

You have seventy general managers in thirty states reporting to a bunch of regional managers. You have three offices in different cities with 120 corporate staff people. You don't have time to make a count, but you must have at least ten lawyers calling you, some on your side, some not.

You miss having direct contact with your guests, and you don't have any exposure to the rich and famous and powerful people you have met on your way to this crummy job.

To cap it all, you have several thousand employees out there who you know are not being trained and led the way you would do it.

Cancel the poolside lunch; just have a club sandwich sent up to the office with a glass of milk for your acid stomach, and hold the scotch and water.

It doesn't take many months for you to see that the people in the field view you as knowing less than when you got out of college. You are in the ivory tower now. What could you possibly know about running hotels or what goes on in them? They expect that you are a slightly pudgy, balding guy sitting in a plush office in a three-piece suit, smoking a pipe and sipping a latte with your feet on a polished mahogany desk. That was my predecessor and he was fired.

Your life isn't that simple. Want me to review your schedule for next week? It won't hurt much; it is just a typical week for you.

You get to the office a 5 a.m. on Monday. You review regional reports and prep a staff meeting for 8 a.m. At 9:30, you are on your way to the airport. At 11 a.m., you are in one of your other offices, prepping for a lunch staff meeting there. You spend part of the afternoon fielding phone calls from lawyers and hotel owners, and some quack who wants your job.

You catch a flight to Chicago for a late dinner meeting with an unhappy hotel owner. After dinner, you rent a car and drive to a hotel that is under construction in Indiana and has union problems.

At 8 a.m. on Tuesday, you are having breakfast with the union business agent and the client, this one is a senior executive of a big trust bank. By 11 a.m., you have fixed the union issues and by noon, you are on a plane to Charleston, South Carolina, for an afternoon meeting with a regional manager who has a drinking problem. That doesn't go well and you fire him. You call your secretary and have her send a memo to his hotel managers, that until further notice they report to you. You catch a 6 p.m. flight to Miami and that evening you tour two of your hotels with the managers and owners.

Wednesday morning, you catch a 5 a.m. flight to NYC for a lunch meeting with a large capital company that is planning to foreclose on three large hotels. By mid-afternoon, all the NYC airports are closed due to snow. You spend the afternoon re-scheduling the rest of your week, returning phone calls, and running proformas on the three hotels.

Thursday morning you fly to Atlanta where you have scheduled a meeting with the General Managers now reporting to you. You hope you can find a replacement Regional Manager among them. You do and catch a 3 p.m. flight to another regional office. Meetings for the rest of that day and evening, then catch a midnight flight back east to your main base. You nap on the plane, change clothes in the plane's restroom and go to the office for more meetings and phone calls, taking up all of Friday.

Saturday you do everything that you didn't do from Monday through Friday, and wade through a small mountain of reports, memos, and letters. Sunday you sleep most of the day and dream about the good old days when you were just a GM. The next week you do some variation of it again.

Somewhere in there, you missed lunch by the pool; in fact, you missed a couple of lunches and several breakfasts completely, and Delta says your luggage is either still in San Francisco or in Seattle; they aren't sure which. My luggage has vacationed in Hawaii several times, but I haven't made it there yet.

Silently over the next few years, more of your hair falls out and the rest turns gray. The doctor puts you on Nexium, since Mylanta doesn't cut it anymore. The bags under your eyes get large enough to plant beans in, you can't get the red out of your eyes, the right one has a periodic tic in it, and you find yourself talking to yourself sometimes.

Death has stalked you through one plane crash and a few near misses. He has hovered in the background through several car wrecks and a couple of life threatening illnesses and a few attacks by employees and guests. Obviously, your angel has warded him off so far.

After a few years of this, you say to hell with this. I've had enough fun for two life times, I'm going to retire, and you do.

You buy some land in the middle of nowhere and build a house in the middle of the land. You lock the gate to your long winding driveway and for two years, you only go out to the grocery once per week. You are people buggy and you don't want to be around them anymore. You spend the next fourteen years sitting in the woods contemplating life and you learn a lot.

You buy a goat, a couple of pot-bellied pigs, two saddle horses, some chickens, geese, ducks, and rabbits. Dumb animals as some would call them. You learn very quickly that these animals are not dumb. They are smarter that some people that you have known. What is even better is they are completely trustworthy, well except for the goat. The goat does have a penchant for butting you into the duck pond when you are not looking. She

also likes to raid your vegetable garden regularly. They don't try
to steal from you. They don't try to hit you over the head with a
lamp or table leg. They are absolutely faithful. All you have to do
is feed them, give them fresh water, and pat them on the head a
couple of times every day. One of the pot-bellied pigs likes to sit
in your lap and eat peanuts out of your hand. Not one animal
tried to commit suicide by jumping off the barn or by blowing
their brains out.

You also enjoy watching the wild life. The birds, rabbits,
squirrels, deer, and if you are lucky a black bear. You soak up the
tranquility and the leisure. You commune with nature and relax.
You need it all.

You learn all over again to sit and enjoy a meal at leisure. No
frantic phone calls, no upset guests. Now if you could just get into
the habit of sleeping past 4 am.

One of the things that you realize is that most of the events and
problems you have endured and that gave you the most
heartburn and consternation were not as important as they
seemed at the time.

Other life lessons come into focus, such as:

People are people. You can't often change them but you can
bend their short-term behavior. You must take them as they are,
as they must take you, warts, and all. Most are good in some
respects and bad in others. You find that you can accept that now
and begin to make some social relationships, but not too close.

Life is short, and your grip on it is tenuous at best. So, you
need to be happy and enjoy it. If you are in a situation that is not
good and you can't fix it, then get out of it. Make a change and do
it before it sours you.

Don't hate anyone and don't hold grudges for real or perceived
hurts. That will only poison your soul.

Life has a way of paying back bad people. You have known
several bad people, some even evil. They have all been paid off at

some point without you having to do it and live with a bad conscience. You have to be able to look yourself in the eye when you shave, or put on make-up.

You have the luxury of reviewing all the bad judgment calls you have made and all the mistakes. If you had done the same thing now, knowing only what you did at the time, would you make the same call? If so, then you should have no regrets and be at peace.

Everything is in the eye of the beholder. Are you rich? Yes, you are, compared to someone who lives in a rented twenty-year-old mobile home, but not compared to a billionaire. Are you healthy? No, not when compared to a twenty-five-year-old athlete, but yes, compared to a person with terminal cancer. It is like the adage, "I felt sorry for myself that I had no shoes, until I met a man who had no feet." Accept your lot in life, do what you can to improve it without hurting others, and be happy.

Like everyone else, you have had some fun, some hurts, some frustrations, some failures, and some successes. Be compassionate to others and be at peace.

As the song says, "Life is a Caberet, old chum, Come to the Cabaret!"

CPSIA information can be obtained at www.ICGtesting.com
Printed in the USA
LVOW040851301011

252690LV00001B/5/P